We *Can* Prevent
World War III

WE CAN PREVENT WORLD WAR III

SAM COHEN

Jameson Books, Inc.

Ottawa, Illinois

Distributed by Kampmann and Company, New York City.

All returns to Kampmann and Co. warehouse.

Jameson books are available at special discounts for bulk purchases for sales promotions, premiums, fund-raising, or educational use. Special editions or book excerpts can also be created to specification.

For details contact:

Special Sales Director
Jameson Books
P.O. Box 738
Ottawa, IL 61350

5 4 3 2 1

Printed in the United States of America

Library of Congress Cataloging in Publication Data

Cohen, S. T.
  We can prevent World War III.

  Bibliography: p.
  Includes index.
  1. Nuclear arms control.   2. Nuclear warfare.
I. Title.
JX1974.7.C54 1985   327.1'74   85-5785
ISBN 0-915463-10-5

To Our Founding Fathers,
who would be appalled.

CONTENTS

INTRODUCTION

CHANCES ARE THAT you are one of a hundred million Americans reported to have seen the ABC nuclear-war movie *The Day After*. Chances are that if you did see the movie, you were one of the large majority of viewers whose opinion on the nuclear-war issue was unaffected by the movie. As reported in the press, most viewers turned off their TV sets still holding to the opinion that we had to make even more concerted efforts to reduce the threat of nuclear war either through arms-control agreements, or through backing President Reagan's defense program, which involved a substantial building up of our military arsenal to be able to counter the Soviet buildup. And chances are that regardless of which side you were on, you never got the critical message of the movie, which was that nuclear war could be caused by factors having nothing to do with arms control or building up our military strength: namely, by factors having to do with the behavior of human beings and the nations they belong to and their continuing propensity to go to war. This goes for the United States, which since World War II has managed to get itself into two major wars overseas because of a national policy that says we are honorbound to protect other countries around the world from communist aggression.

You'll recall that *The Day After* came about because, once again, Europe embroiled itself in conflict: this time between East Germany (a Soviet military ally) and West Germany (an American military ally). And before you knew it the Red Army, coming to the aid of the Soviet's Warsaw Pact ally, was invading Western Europe, where the United States had stationed more than 200,000 soldiers to protect its NATO allies. Since the Red Army always has had conventional capabilities superior to those of NATO, it quickly succeeded in its assault; the United States, loyally keeping its pledge to NATO allies, had to use tactical nuclear weapons to stem

1

the tide. Whereupon, the nuclear threshold having been crossed, the situation rapidly got out of hand and the U.S. came under Soviet nuclear attack, with Lawrence, Kansas, being the TV camera's focal point to show what can happen to a city near U.S. nuclear missile bases that are targets for Russian nuclear missiles. What happened was, of course, horrendous.

It happened not because we had failed to consummate arms-control treaties or to achieve President Reagan's proposed military buildup. It happened because people and nations went on behaving like people and nations, but this time in an age of thousands of nuclear weapons, which were used for the above-mentioned reasons: people and nations haven't changed and the United States, through its policy of military intervention around the world, had put itself into a position where it couldn't avoid being drawn into a war that became a nuclear war. This was the critical message of *The Day After*: if we really want to avoid nuclear war, the best way to do so is to stop ourselves from getting into confrontations overseas that can lead to this horrible result. In this respect, I might say that the scenario of *The Day After* was not at all unrealistic. Having been in the nuclear-war business for almost forty years, I have seen our war gamers play out this scenario, or one akin to it, many times. If one chooses to dismiss this scenario as little more than a fantasy, since nuclear war frequently is dismissed as "unthinkable," all I can say is that our nuclear-policy planners have not. To the contrary, they long have taken this kind of scenario very seriously.

How many Americans picked up this critical message while watching the movie, I don't know; but I suspect precious few, for most Americans have tended to place blind trust in their government's national security policies, which have been providing less and less security as Soviet nuclear capabilities have increased. Most Americans have told themselves that our nuclear policies are far too complex for them to grasp and decided that their government's policies were best representing their interests. This has not been the case, and *The Day After* makes this very clear in showing how nuclear war is distinctly possible and why. The truth of the matter is that our national security policies have not been based on the real world of people and nations. Had they been so, they would have been extremely simple for Americans to grasp, for the simple reason that they would have been based on the supreme national interest of our country, which the Constitution says is providing our "common defense" and to "secure the blessings of liberty to ourselves and our posterity." Most Americans still believe in our Constitution.

But our government has not been doing this for the American people. Instead it has been spending the great bulk of its defense budget on attempting to defend other countries and essentially nothing on defending our own country from nuclear attack. There is something terribly wrong about the way we go about attaining our national security objectives, the most vital by far being the avoidance of nuclear war. We have blindly and dangerously persisted in a policy of intervention in foreign wars, a policy which holds the greatest probability that one of these wars will come to our own doorstep—with nuclear weapons. And should this happen, unless we take measures to change our unrealistic policies, our liberty and our posterity will come to a tragic ending.

Another message strongly implicit in *The Day After* is that of the need for defense of our country. Had the government provided the people of Lawrence with an effective civil defense and established an antimissile system around the U.S. missile field near Lawrence, very probably the horror could have been prevented or drastically alleviated, and the movie would have had a much different complexion. However, far more important, if the government had changed its policy of military intervention to one of defending the United States, the scenario of *The Day After* would not have been possible and the only kind of movie that could have been produced would have been a colossal flop; and so it wouldn't have been produced in the first place.

This book attempts to explain to the American people the real danger of nuclear war; how we can best avoid it; and if it comes anyway, despite our best efforts to avoid it, how we can survive as a free nation with a meaningful future. As you will read, I find our country's defense policies to be wrong and dangerous. However, my faultfinding is based not on a worldview shaped by personal biases and fantasies, but on more than thirty-five years of professional experience in all aspects of nuclear war, aspects that necessitated my being aware of all the official data on which our official policies are based. As such, the proposals I make here for avoiding and surviving nuclear war result not from imagination, but from the information our government has supplied to the Congress and the American people. So if I find fault with our government's policies it is because, for political reasons, the government has been at odds with itself in not objectively using its own information.

3

When queried over the years, the American people overwhelmingly have been in favor of defense against nuclear attack and have indicated a willingness to pay the price for their protection. The trouble has been that whenever U.S. presidents have proposed such protection, enormous political pressures—generated by the media and powerful antinuclear groups having great influence on the media—have been directed against them, forcing them to back away. And when that has happened, the American people have remained virtually mute on the sidelines, in confusion over whom to believe.

Worse yet, over the years there have been conscious and deliberate policy decisions by U.S. administrations to emasculate what defenses existed and deny the possibility of establishing effective defenses. (Take, for example, the antiballistic missile [ABM] treaty of 1972, signed with the USSR, which forbade the U.S. to defend itself against Soviet ballistic missile attack; that treaty was signed soon after President Nixon had declared: "No president with the responsibility for the lives and security of the American people could fail to provide this protection.")

Instead, our government has held to policies that involve spending the bulk of its defense money toward defending with conventional forces countries around the world that appear threatened by the Soviet Union or its communist surrogates—countries where thus far our record has been notoriously unsuccessful and where we will be courting disaster, including nuclear war, if we continue down this path.

At the same time, the government has been fashioning nuclear forces that actually are incapable of fighting a nuclear war and of reducing the carnage and devastation to the American people. A prime example is the MX missile. And while all this has been going on, the American people have remained passive, holding faith, however unwarranted it may be, in the wisdom of their government, however lacking this quality has been in our government.

If our country is to survive the perils of the nuclear age, it can come about only if the American people come out of their cocoon of ignorance and apathy, attempt to understand what the issues really are (which can be easily done because the issues are basically simple), and fight back—for their lives. Their future will be best secured rather by demanding it from their government than by proceeding on the faith that their government is acting in their best security interests, which may not be the case.

4

1

Will There Be Nuclear War?

> We sit by and watch the Barbarian, we tolerate him: in the
> long stretches of peace we are not afraid. We are tickled by
> his irreverence; his comic inversion of our old certitudes
> and our fixed creeds refreshes us: we laugh. But as we laugh
> we are watched by large and awful faces from beyond: and
> on these faces there is no smile.
>
> Hilaire Belloc

SHORTLY BEFORE DAWN on 12 August 1958 I stood on the deck
of an aircraft carrier some seven hundred miles southwest of Hon-
olulu, my back turned to a multimegaton nuclear warhead about
to go off at an altitude of more than twenty-five miles. I already
had witnessed high-yield nuclear tests and by now had become
used to the spectacle. Although I knew technically that this was
going to be something different, my expectation was based on the
saying, from experience: "If you've seen one, you've seen 'em all."
But this wasn't to be the case.

   As had happened previously, the area around me suddenly was
bathed in extremely bright white, and I began to feel very warm
from the radiant energy pouring out of the explosion. When I
turned around, however, some seconds later, and when I could
look without hurting my eyes, there was something I had never
seen before. An enormous, silent, baleful, yellow-green radioluminescent face covered most of the sky above me.

5

Everyone on deck was equally silent, staring at the face that beheld us as the terrifying spectacle unfolded. Many minutes later we were jolted out of our muteness when the blast wave finally hit; whereupon the air force colonel standing next to me exclaimed: "There can't be a nuclear war; there just can't be one!" I suspect the colonel was wrong then. Were he to repeat himself today, he would be terribly wrong; for today we are heading irrationally and lemminglike toward nuclear war.

Some folk, all well meaning and many highly intelligent, believe that the way to cure ourselves of warlike habits is to dig into the causes of such habits. We're a rational species and if we can understand why we do irrational things, we'll simply stop doing them.

Historically oriented types suggest that to prevent the next war from happening we must analyze, going backward in time, the series of human events and conditions that led up to previous wars and look for common denominators to be able to sense the next one in the making and thereby take steps to avoid it. (In France is a group that does this sort of thing. The members call themselves polymologists, and they work a few hundred feet from Napoleon's tomb. When I asked them a few years ago if their analysis of current events and conditions predicted World War III, the answer was: "Monsieur, it has already begun; the bombs haven't dropped yet.") One unchanging characteristic of human beings has been their propensity to go to war. However, awareness of such a shabby history has accomplished little to prevent it from repeating itself.

Many see a dollar sign behind many a war. Nations fight for economic gain or to avoid economic loss. It's as simple as all that. Which supposedly explains why the United States has been willing to fight all over the world for its so-called vital interests—spelled *money*—even though our national bank account has gone deeply into the red with each war we've fought.

Others, less materialistically inclined, ascribe our willingness to fight to such lofty motives as honor, decency, integrity, loyalty, self-esteem, and the like. These are the qualities that make up the spiritual well-being of our nation, and that move us to dedicate ourselves to the well-being of fellow humans around the world. Without these qualities our lives would not be worth living, even though we often tend to dismiss them in dealing among ourselves. However, assuming that our involvement in wars has indeed improved the well-being of other countries, some of us judge that it

6

has proved to be a pretty transient business, as those countries set about preparing for the next war and then participating in it.

Then there are the real basic types, those that get down to the nitty-gritty of man the animal. We're driven by instincts, say they, and some of them drive us into war. Atop most instinct lists is aggressiveness. We have strong urges to beat out the brains of our fellows, and a nation's doing it occasionally to another nation makes darned good excitement. Something like that a man can rejoice over, and his children can glory in the war stories, if his side has won.

Another instinct underlying conflict, say the real basic types, is sexual competition between males. Unquestionably, that is behind the organized conflict in what we humans of great intellect like to call lower forms of life. Older men, having less sex drive but greater wiliness and political power than the young males with whom they compete, ingeniously contrive conditions that cause war and then send forth the young males to kill or be killed while they take the excess of available females (mainly younger and more attractive than their wives) for themselves.

Another school of thought says, in effect: Forget about trying to explain war; accept it as a fact of life that always has been with us, and will be with us forever. So get with it, says this school, and start thinking about World War IV and V; that's the real world! These gentle folk may have more going for their position than any others; they're certainly more into the real world than the rest. They're certainly more consonant with our current defense policies, which make war increasingly probable. But one thing worries me about their position: that enormous radioluminescent face that looked down on me that morning. I wouldn't care to see thousands of such faces appearing over my country, watching it disappear because it had laughed at Belloc's Barbarian, knowing with certitude that he had become too horrible to be released: spelled *nuclear deterrence.*

It's hard to quarrel with the historically oriented types who search for causes (that is, conditions) of war (like the polymologists in France), because they have all the facts on their side—namely, what's already happened on the human scene before war breaks out. However, they are fatalists; they say it's going to happen again because of recurrent conditions that made it happen before. They have left out the one human factor that allows us to hope we can avoid nuclear war: free will. Which may not be worth very much because we're not really all that free, but it's still our only hope.

As for those who cite economic imperatives, those "vital interests" of the United States, they're pathetically wrong. Let them name just one major war we've been in that didn't put us into the red. Here's roughly what the wars we've fought this century have cost us (in 1983 dollars): World War I—$400 billion; World War II—$2 trillion; Korea (we didn't even win)—$300 billion; Vietnam (we lost)—$400 billion. And after the first three of those wars, we poured out billions and billions of dollars to help the countries we both saved and defeated get back on their feet. What did we gain from all this? The toughest, most ruthless economic competition we've ever had, which is pushing us toward economic isolationism. If we accept the economic argument at face value, we ought to go into both economic and military isolationism—especially the latter, which really can protect our vital interests, our pocketbook.

What about the ideologists, those self-appointed spiritual policemen of the free world who believe that God singled out our great nation to fulfill this role in the world today? They should take a look at the record. In World War I we helped the French and English protect their freedom against the Huns, only to see them sit on their hands while Hitler began enslaving countries right and left, finally gobbling up France in World War II and coming close to doing the same to England. Our great democratic European allies showed little appreciation for our noblesse oblige in World War I, greedily enhancing their national interests as soon as the war was over, and making us look like noble idiots. In World War II, which we entered because war was declared on us, we freed the Chinese from the barbaric Japanese, only to see, a few years later, China come under a far worse slavery than they had experienced under the Japanese, and shortly after that start to kill American soldiers in Korea. As for the Japanese, our mortal enemies in World War II, who used Americans as scientific guinea pigs for proof-testing their weapons, we wound up actually freeing them from despotism by firebombing and A-bombing their cities to bring about their surrender. They are now a great thriving democracy and a close ally that we're willing to defend to our themonuclear death. And what did all our ideology gain us in Vietnam? For these reasons, when I hear our fearless leaders explain our massive buildup of conventional forces, which eat up close to nine of ten defense dollars, as being necessary to preserve freedom around the world, my stomach begins to churn.

Those who dwell on our basic instincts fail to explain satisfactorily why we cannot so control ourselves as not to yield to our

8

aggressive impulses to kill and maim millions of people halfway around the world, even though we manage, within reason, to control ourselves back home where it is far easier to indulge in such mayhem. And then there's sex—virtually the basest of instincts when I was a youngster, but now the only noble one in our liberated times, which reminds me of an anecdote that may be the best reflection of all on war:

A young man is about to take his girlfriend out on his boat for the weekend. To prepare against two potential undesirable eventualities, he checks in at a drugstore and orders a box of prophylactics and a bottle of Dramamine. The druggist returns with the order and asks, "If it makes you sick to do it, why do you do it?"

The last time we went to war (in Vietnam) we really became sick. It was a fruitless, humiliating experience that we vowed never to repeat. From now on, declared Richard Nixon in 1969, in announcing his (briefly) famous Nixon doctrine for Asia, Asian wars are going to have to be fought by Asians. We'll sell them all the military hardware they need (which does make good economic sense) for their defense; which is why we're up to our ears in the Merchants of Death business. But no more American boys will be sent to Asia to fight and die. Sounded great to Americans who were fed up to their ears with war; and Nixon was declared a foreign policy guru by them, and many others. In fact, we were so sick of war that when South Vietnam fell most of us just shrugged it off. President Ford was on vacation in Palm Springs playing golf.

But that was a long time ago. Just look at what's going on today. We're preparing to spend about $1.5 *trillion* during this decade on our conventional forces, to be able to fight not only another ground war in Asia, but a war wherever else we fear the Russians may be up to no good. Listen to how Defense Secretary Caspar Weinberger explained the need for this buildup:

> Conventional wars could come in all sizes; if we value our freedom, we must be able to defend ourselves in wars of any size and shape and in any region where we have vital interests. That means developing urgently a better ability to respond to crises far from our shores, and to stay there as long as necessary. The West's dependence on [Persian Gulf] oil means that we must make sure we can respond effectively to threats in this region.[1]

A few years ago I listened to an assistant secretary of defense back up his boss's explanation for expanding U.S. conventional forces. This fellow singled out preserving the flow of Persian Gulf oil as the primary reason for developing our Rapid Deployment Force (RDF). Keeping the Gulf oil flowing was in the most vital of our vital interests in Asia and we had no choice but to foot the bill for the RDF, whatever the price. (He didn't explain why *we* had to shell out all this money, while our European and Japanese allies, who need the oil far more than we, sat by and cheered us on in this enterprise. Nor why *we* were required to send hundreds of thousands of U.S. boys over there to get shot up protecting *their* needs.) His estimate of the cost of fighting the Russians over there was well in excess of a trillion dollars a year. A high price, sure; but grimly necessary, because of our "vital interests." Baloney!

The Persian Gulf pumps about ten million barrels of oil a day and has been charging roughly $30 a barrel in recent years. If we multiply these numbers and then multiply the result by the number of days in a year, the product is on the order of $100 billion. A lot of money, to be sure; but very little compared with the yearly price (maybe trillions of dollars) of our fighting to save oil for Europe and Japan, and profits for the Saudis. And this leaves out the cost in blood of American soldiers, not to mention the incalculable amount of bloodshed back home should the Gulf war escalate to nuclear war between us and Russia—and well it might, once the passions surrounding war break loose. Our *real* vital interests ought to be our own national survival, but we seldom pause to think about that, and how we're actually risking what we're trying to preserve.

What I've just described has to be the most dangerous and ir-rational form of behavior a nation can take. But that's what we're up to and very few pay serious attention to what's going on, even though our survival is at stake. With ease our country can survive without Gulf oil; with ease our country can perish in a nuclear war brought about by fighting in the Persian Gulf.

Incidentally, why is it that the government, in trying to justify the need for the RDF, assumes that the Russians covet Gulf oil enough to want to risk going to war with us? They certainly don't need it for themselves. The USSR is the world's biggest oil pro-ducer; it exports the stuff. If the Soviets want to deny it to the West, all they have to do is to threaten Gulf shipping. Insurance rates will go through the ceiling and tankers will stop going there. Or if the Soviets felt compelled to make a show of military force to stop the oil flow, they could dispatch some bombers or missiles to the oil refineries and cover them with some chemical agent, as they've been doing in Afghanistan. What could we do to counter this? Attack the Soviet Union directly and start World War III?

We really have gone out of our minds; that is, unless we're unwittingly playing another game of war, whose rules are made by Belloc's awful faces. And our departure from military reality is not confined to containing the Soviets in Asia. The situation in Europe is just as irrational, maybe even more so, and certainly more dangerous, because we're more committed.

The NATO allies, including the U.S., have postured and trained their forces to refight World War II with conventional armies. Although we are now almost forty years into the nuclear age, NATO's policy rejects the use of nuclear weapons to achieve policy objectives (for example, hold back the Red Army); its forces are not trained in nuclear warfare; and its nuclear weapons, almost all of them belonging to the United States, are based on a strategy intended mainly to ensure that their use will envelop the United States and the Soviet Union in a thermonuclear exchange. In other words, we have developed and deployed nuclear weapons for NATO whose use may succeed in killing us. Our nuclear weapons, supposedly intended to protect Europeans, are actually, by our own policy, directed toward our own suicide.

This is the bedrock of NATO's deterrent strategy: our threat to commit suicide. Our European allies are not really interested in putting up a fight to keep out the Red Army. They have yet to muster up the forces to be able to fight a ground war in their own defense. Rather, as Henry Kissinger explained several years ago: "The secret dream of many Europeans was, of course, to avoid a nuclear war, but . . . if there had to be a nuclear war, to have it conducted over their heads by the strategic forces of the United States and the Soviet Union."[2]

Why has the U.S. government tolerated this state of affairs? Why haven't the American people, especially those who are particularly terrified of nuclear extermination and join antinuclear and nuclear-freeze movements, recognized what their government stands ready to do to them, and demanded that this insanity immediately end? Don't they realize that Europe's history has been continually marked by irrational wars? The last two we were drawn into and survived, but the next one we get into may kill us if we don't quit the mess that we created.

They would if they just took the time—not all that much time—to reflect on this; but so far they have not. Even though for the first time in our national history our supreme national interests, our physical survival, are directly at stake, we act as though the world had not really changed. As usual, "we sit by and watch the Barbarian," who now can kill us. The world has changed fantastically with the existence of nuclear weapons, and we still can't look into those awful faces of Belloc to see what we are doing to ourselves. We still can't look into ourselves. Probably for fear of finding out who we really are, and still not being able to do anything about it.

The Soviets know who we are, who they are, and who the Barbarian is in the nuclear age. They have not forgotten Lenin's admonition that peace is but a respite between wars. Their doctrine for war with NATO is not a repetition of World War II; rather it is based on "the decisive form of military action" that nuclear weapons can provide; and they equip, train, and exercise their troops accordingly. They acknowledge that the world has changed dramatically because of nuclear weapons; but, unlike the West, they do not reject these weapons for fighting wars to achieve policy objectives. To the contrary, they hold to the belief that "the relationship between politics and war, thoroughly revealed in the writings of Lenin, not only remains valid in the nuclear age, but acquires even greater significance."[3] Our Defense Department long has acknowledged and officially confirmed this Soviet viewpoint.

On what rational basis would the Soviets want to ignore their massive nuclear preparations and chance a conventional war to oblige NATO's conventional preparations? Two renowned U.S. strategists long ago maintained that they would not: Henry Kissinger, who does not have to be introduced, stated: "Regardless of what we may decide, the Soviets may introduce nuclear weapons first; in fact, if they have not lost their senses, they almost have to use nuclear weapons first."[4] Bernard Brodie, a former colleague of Kissinger and author of the first definitive tract on nuclear strategy, declared: "Can anyone believe, with confidence, that the Soviet Union would challenge us to so deadly a duel and yet leave the choice of weapons entirely to us? Can anyone seriously think that if the Russians launched such an attack, they would not be determined to win it as quickly as possible by offensive action, with whatever weapons were necessary to accomplish that victory?"[5]

Yet, in the face of all this, we continue to prepare only for a big conventional war in Europe. Clearly, this is no way to win, but clearly this is the only way we're willing to fight—irrational as this may be. And to make sure that we can keep our troops over there to be able to fight, even though they'll be wiped out, we go on mouthing these banalities about vital interests, spiritual needs, honor, pride, and other nonsense.

Infrequently a few congressmen complain mildly that keeping our conventional forces in Europe is costing too much money, that our European allies aren't footing their fair share of the bill, and that we should bring a few thousand American boys back home. When this happens, they are properly reprimanded by the president, the State Department, the Defense Department, the foreign policy establishment, and the "responsible" media; and they back away. But never do they seriously question why our forces are still there, forty years after World War II ended; for that would be to question what this country is all about—like, say, a war machine, despite our pious protestations to the contrary.

If our strategy for a conventional confrontation with the Russians holds a real risk for getting into a nuclear war with them, why are we taking so many conventional-force measures (at such tremendous expense) that may get us into such a predicament?* Which brings us back to why we want to do such things as going to war, in the first place. And this again prompts the question of what motivates us in this irrational direction: namely, who are we? Or what are we? Is there somewhere in our collective unconscious a rational (as nature would look at it) design that has always driven us into war, to meet some biological necessity? Are the large and awful faces not from beyond but from within our germ plasm, dictating our actions like a computer programming a robot? Maybe so, since our basic intelligence hasn't changed to speak of during recorded history; and history includes a record of countless wars. And not only has the human race survived all these thousands of years of conflict, but it has expanded and progressed, from war to war—maybe, as some of the Darwinian types might argue, because of war.

So why don't we just go on our merry way, as we always have? Damn the pricetag; whatever it is, we've got to be prepared to fight to maintain world order (the most appalling, rarely noted, contradiction of all). Life without honor is not worth living, and if our

* In 1983 the celebrated Scowcroft commission, a bipartisan group of renowned foreign policy and defense "experts" (including former secretaries of state and defense) established by President Reagan, issued a report, which stated: ". . . conventional war between the world's major power blocs is the most likely way for nuclear war to develop. The problem of deterring the threat of nuclear war, in short, cannot be isolated from the overall power balance between East and West. Simply put, it is war that must concern us, not nuclear war alone."

13

soldiers have to die somewhere overseas for our honor, that's worth it. Except if we keep this up very much longer and stand ready to challenge the Russians at every turn, the order we once again seek to maintain will once again turn into military disorder. This time, however, it will most likely be *nuclear* disorder. In which case our soldiers may have died for our national honor, but at the same time our honor will have cost us our national existence. Is this worth risking?

John Quincy Adams said, "America must be the friend of liberty everywhere, but bear the responsibility only for its own." But as the current wisdom of the U.S. foreign policy establishment has it, World War II and the events leading up to it have proved without a doubt that Adams was wrong. America today has no responsible choice but to help protect the liberty of other nations. This is the essence of our containment policy, which was established right after World War II, and which purports to prevent communism, especially Soviet communism, from enslaving the free world. However, today two fundamental flaws sully this policy.

First, those nations whose liberty we vowed to protect some four decades ago are now mostly capable of protecting themselves. Their economic and social prostration of the late 1940s is long gone. Today they have the money, the industrial resources, the technology, and the manpower to assume the responsibility for their own defenses. So why must this remain our responsibility?

Second, when our containment policy was established we held a monopoly of nuclear weapons and for many years after we could threaten the Soviets with nuclear devastation if they threatened the liberty of our allies. Today, however, our nuclear superiority is gone and if we are to make nuclear threats against the Soviets if they threaten our friends and allies, we are threatening only our own destruction. What we call "extended nuclear deterrence," in the parlance of modern strategists, has now become self-deterring—unless our implicit policy is self-destruction, which it seems to be. Our nuclear guarantees to allies now promise to save neither their liberty nor ours. So why must we hold to such a dangerous and irresponsible policy?

If we continue to hold to military policies out of the past, with all the glory and excitement of sending our troops overseas to kill and be killed, one of these days our future may abruptly end. Lord Tennyson once described the *raison d'être* of a good British soldier: "Theirs not to reason why, theirs is but do and die." American

14

boys make good soldiers, they always have, and they'll go if they're ordered overseas to fight once again. But in an age of intercontinental nuclear missiles, overseas for them is back here for us. So maybe we, the American people, should start to reason why, because back here we'll only die; we won't be able to cheer our boys on over there. The American people had better begin to reason; their fearless leaders in Washington apparently won't, because they're so damned fearless—and unreasoning.

Bernard Brodie once observed: "It is an old story that one way of keeping people out of trouble is to deny them the means of getting into it." One way of keeping ourselves out of wars around the world is to deny ourselves the means of fighting such wars. Nothing could be more simple: bring home our troops now overseas, put them into mufti, and sell as much of their equipment as is needed to the countries they leave so that those countries can defend themselves. At the same time, we should disband our plans for deploying forces overseas in the event of war there to make sure that if we're tempted to revert to past behavior, we won't be able to do so. And then we must begin to think, for a change, about how we can defend our own liberty back here.

Will there be a nuclear war? Probably; almost undoubtedly. Unless we come to our senses and change our warlike ways for preserving the peace.

2

Can We Fight the Red Army?

IN 1975, FOR THE FIRST TIME, the U.S. Defense Department revealed how the Soviet Union viewed its nuclear weapons in the event of a ground war with NATO. This came out in a report to the Congress by Defense Secretary James Schlesinger, entitled "The Theater Nuclear Force Posture in Europe." What Schlesinger said should have badly shaken Congress (which had requested the report) for he told it, in effect, that it was spending the American taxpayers' money, then and now involving about half the U.S. defense budget, to prepare for a war in Europe that most likely wouldn't happen. It should have shaken the American taxpayers, had they bothered to read it. But then, this matter is something over which the American taxpayers have seldom bothered to concern themselves, even though it directly affects their state of financial health, to say nothing of their survival should NATO have to fight the Red Army.

NATO, for more than a dozen years, had been spending most of its money and structuring its forces to defend conventionally against an expected conventional-weapon attack by the Soviets and their Warsaw Pact allies. Moreover, NATO policy, shaped almost exclusively by the United States, had assumed that the Soviets would prefer to keep the war conventional and, if possible, effect a settlement without having to use nuclear weapons. The first use

16

of tactical nuclear weapons would be a U.S. option (practically all these weapons being U.S.-owned), not a Soviet option; and such use would come only if NATO's conventional defenses were on the verge of collapse, after days or weeks of conventional battle.

Since it was (and still is) NATO's official position that the Soviet-bloc conventional forces were far more powerful than those of NATO, it was (and still is) anticipated that NATO's first nuclear-use option would have to be exercised. This would involve the use of battlefield nuclear weapons. In fact, at the time his report was issued, Schlesinger already had ordered the development of neutron warheads to make these weapons more effective and more discriminating. But it was clearly understood, for NATO policy, that these were weapons primarily of last resort, to avoid conventional defeat. They were not regarded as a serious military response to a Soviet first use of nuclear weapons, which U.S. policy had ruled out. Moreover, U.S. forces are not realistically trained in the use of battlefield nuclear weapons, nor does an underlying military doctrine exist for such use.

According to Schlesinger (more accurately, according to the Pentagon's intelligence assessment of the Soviets), there was little likelihood that Soviet military doctrine was at all obliging of U.S. policy: "While there are indications that the Warsaw Pact strategists have accepted the concept of a possible initial conventional phase, Warsaw Pact forces are in fact postured and trained for theaterwide nuclear strikes against NATO nuclear and conventional military forces and for follow-on attacks by their armored conventional forces to exploit the nuclear attack and rapidly seize NATO territory." In other words, the Warsaw Pact forces (tightly controlled by Moscow) had geared themselves to fight a nuclear war in Europe and expected to use their nuclear weapons early in a conflict; perhaps at the very beginning, in accordance with the emphasis their doctrine places on nuclear surprise and preemptive attacks (brought out in Schlesinger's report).

To give more credence to U.S. nuclear-weapon capabilities in NATO, Schlesinger directed a long overdue program of modernization of these weapons. They were to be more survivable against a Soviet nuclear attack; their command and control, should they have to be used in numbers over a period of time, were to be substantially improved; and priority was given to achieving more discriminate means of nuclear attack.

Since these directives were issued, nothing of real substance has been accomplished in the first two categories. The weapons are just about as survivable (or nonsurvivable) today as they were in 1975; and just about as controllable (or noncontrollable). Which is not an oversight, since our regard for nuclear weapons to be used in actual ground combat has eroded consistently over these years; with current plans in effect to reduce significantly the number of these weapons in Europe. In the third category, greater discrimination, only *one* improvement was made—the neutron bomb. But consider the fate of this one improvement.

Writing to Senator John Stennis in July 1977, President Carter declared the neutron bomb to be "in this nation's security interest. I therefore urge Congress to approve the current funding request." Congress, by a large majority, gave the president the support he asked for; but not so our NATO allies. Over much of Europe, our attempt to force the neutron bomb on NATO touched off widespread popular demonstrations and political divisiveness. In the end, even though there was a begrudging acceptance by most NATO European nations, Carter chose to back away and defer on production, which he did to the expiration of his term; and probably would have continued to do so had he been reelected.

In early 1981 the Reagan administration, through Defense Secretary Caspar Weinberger, served notice of its intention to produce neutron warheads. Said Weinberger: "When you look at the number of Russian tanks and the other items, the [neutron] warhead would do quite a lot to restore some kind of balance there." The result of Weinberger's declaration was a deep split in the administration, the State Department fearing that this would ruffle our allies' feathers. And there was an unofficial rejection of these weapons by our allies, indicating that indeed their feathers had been ruffled. When President Reagan announced his decision, in August 1981, to produce neutron warheads, their rejection by the allies became apparent: the warheads would not be stockpiled in Europe. What also became apparent was that the Europeans for some time had rejected *all* battlefield weapons as a meaningful response to an overwhelming conventional attack. They simply were not interested in nuclear war being fought on their territory. So our neutron bombs are now being stored on U.S. soil, where they are of no use to anyone, including the United States. Which makes one wonder why they are being produced at all.

Throughout the neutron-bomb episode, there was hardly a mention of the role that NATO's conventional weapons might play in beating back a Warsaw Pact conventional attack. Implied by this silence seemed to be an admission that advanced conventional-weapon developments did not offer realistic hopes for neutralizing the huge Pact conventional-force advantage. (Certainly the current conventional weapons at hand offered little hope.) Were there to be any chance to resist a Pact armored thrust to the Rhine, it was made clear by U.S. officials that nuclear weapons, particularly the battlefield variety, would be required. However, as a result of the European rejection of neutron warheads, the fate of these weapons, particularly the shorter-range weapons, which most likely would impact on Western European soil, appeared to be hanging in the balance. And since these weapons had been deemed by the United States to be absolutely essential to Europe's defense, the fate of Europe also appeared to be hanging in the balance. Not a very satisfactory situation for the United States, which had conceived and created NATO, and one, if allowed to persist, that might very well endanger the Alliance. And this was absolutely unthinkable, even though there was abundant evidence that staying in the Alliance was increasingly endangering the United States.

In the United States, in certain quarters of the defense establishment, concern began to mount over maintaining NATO's military viability. Was there any way in which longer-range nuclear weapons might be used against Warsaw Pact forces in Eastern Europe in a manner that would have a decisive impact on slowing down and even halting the conventional advance into Western Europe? If this could be accomplished, NATO's future military viability could be ensured and the European allies, especially the West Germans, could be assured that battlefield nuclear weapons would not have to be used on their soil. An impending crisis could be dealt with; the Alliance could be saved.

For some years before the time this question was addressed, Warsaw Pact field exercises had been observed. From these observations came a verification of the basic Soviet military doctrine for its ground armored forces. This doctrine was based on the mounting of successive waves of all-out blitzkrieg attacks against the NATO defenses. When the first wave had been slowed down or seriously attrited, the next wave, coming from the "second-echelon" forces to the rear, would move up to continue the assault. If the second-echelon forces became bogged down, the third echelon, originally based farther to the rear, would move up to join the fray.

The Soviets, it was argued by many who had analyzed the field exercises, had cast their strategy in concrete by repeating this pattern of attack time after time. They would find it extremely difficult, in the event of war, to change this pattern without seriously disrupting the operational effectiveness of their armed forces. Ergo, apparently without knowing it, the Soviets had become potentially vulnerable to a revised NATO strategy based on obtaining a capability to find and destroy their rear-echelon forces in Eastern Europe with tactical nuclear weapons. Were the United States to achieve this capability, the Soviet game plan would become a disaster. And having become irrevocably committed to it, they, obviously, wouldn't dare attack.

Never mind the U.S. assumption that the Soviets would be self-paralyzed and willing to stand by and watch this capability be developed, and propagandized to the world while this was under way, without at least trying to change their strategy. By fiat of these U.S. analysts, the Soviets would find it virtually impossible to extricate themselves from their doctrinal concrete. They now would have to admit to themselves that the enormous military machine they had built up over the years—far more powerful than NATO's and with a more modern, more effective arsenal of nuclear weapons—had been all in vain. The Russian bear would have turned out to be one very dumb animal.

This so-called second-echelon attack strategy could only be credible if a means existed to detect and locate Soviet tank units many tens of miles behind the front line. In the past, gaining such a target-acquisition capability had posed an enormous technical challenge that never had been met. As a result, U.S. battlefield nuclear-weapon strategy had been based on finding the front-line Russian forces very close in where they could be "eyeballed" by target spotters and attacked by quickly responsive nuclear systems, such as artillery. But now suddenly a veritable technical breakthrough seemed at hand, in the form of a new airborne radar that could detect moving armored units at substantial ranges; up to a hundred miles or so. This meant that the Soviet second-echelon units could be found and attacked by longer-range nuclear weapons (such as cruise missiles) on *enemy* soil. A threatening situation now could be defused; the Alliance could go on—not necessarily serenely, but at least out of danger.

This nuclear solution, however, had come too late. By now the NATO Europeans, especially the West Germans, were becoming restive over any kind of battlefield nuclear weapons fired from their soil, regardless of where they might impact. Mounting were their fears of nuclear war restricted to Europe, fears that had been exacerbated by remarks made by President Reagan indicating a limited-theater nuclear war was possible. And the burgeoning antinuclear movement was demanding the removal of *all* nuclear weapons from Europe. It began to look as though no nuclear solution would be acceptable in European eyes; and, once again, the Alliance seemed in jeopardy.

During the late 1970s a group of U.S. military analysts and technologists, who favored removing U.S. battlefield nuclear weapons from Europe, began to examine possibilities for using conventional weapons for attacking second-echelon armored forces as they advanced toward the front lines. Using the new airborne moving-target indicator radars to locate these forces, they assessed the effectiveness of advanced conventional munitions having very precise guidance. The munitions, delivered by aircraft or surface-to-surface missiles, would employ heat-seeking (infrared) devices enabling them to home in on the heat from the tank engines and burst atop the tanks, where the armor is thinnest. Upon bursting, jets of metal would be driven through the relatively thin top armor and wreak havoc upon crew and equipment inside.

To be more specific on how these weapons work, each bomb or missile warhead could contain large numbers of bomblets, called submunitions. The bomblets would be dispersed over the area believed to be occupied by an enemy tank unit. Each bomblet would have heat-seeking guidance equipment to steer it toward the tank below. In contrast to precision-guided antitank weapons thus far developed, where one weapon is directed toward one target, these weapons were designed to cover an area occupied by a number of targets, thus earning them the title "area munitions." It was estimated that taking the area-munition route could lower the tonnage of weapons previously required by perhaps as much as tenfold. It also was estimated that a ton of these area munitions could be almost as effective as a neutron warhead in neutralizing a Soviet tank formation.

By 1982 a number of U.S. and NATO officials had become sufficiently worried about NATO's deteriorating condition as to advance a new doctrine embracing these new conventional-weapon prospects. Implementing this new doctrine, it was argued, would make possible the effective neutralization of the Warsaw Pact's large conventional advantage. They unveiled and gave full publicity to this doctrine. Moving away from NATO's fixed battle-line conventional-war strategy that traced to World War II, they now advanced a strategy emphasizing tactics of maneuver, concealment, and surprise. Added to this, utilizing the new conventional-weapon and deep-target acquisition technology, was the intensive attack of enemy second-echelon units.

Were NATO, said U.S. officials, to commit a mere 1 percent more to the 3 percent budget increase it had pledged to undertake, it could incorporate this new technology into the new strategy and pull even with the Warsaw Pact conventional forces. NATO thereby could achieve its long sought goal of conventional deterrence. Were this to be accomplished, the need to use NATO's battlefield nuclear weapons effectively would diminish greatly—to the great relief of Europeans and Americans as well, since the use of these weapons held the high risk of escalating to strategic nuclear war.

One of the first to expose and explain the implications of the new doctrine and technology was Gen. Bernard Rogers (U.S. Army), supreme allied commander of Europe. General Rogers succinctly summarized the profound implications of attaining such greatly improved NATO conventional forces: "The provision of such a robust conventional capability for NATO not only would enhance deterrence and raise the nuclear threshold, but would face the Warsaw Pact—should it attack conventionally and its attack be frustrated—with either having to be the first to escalate to theater nuclear weapons or withdrawing its forces. Faced with that prospect, I do not believe Soviet leaders would initiate aggression. I believe they are no more anxious than NATO to escalate and cross the nuclear threshold. . . ."[1] Rogers was joined by a number of key U.S. congressmen. The West Germans, who would be expected to bear the brunt of the battle in the event of a Soviet invasion, enthusiastically came aboard; understandably so, since the main NATO military effort now would be against enemy forces in Warsaw Pact territory. The ranks of the second-echelon attack concept continue to expand.

That all this might be little more than pie in the sky and mainly a political gambit never seemed to occur to those being bombarded by these bold claims for this new concept. Doubts that it might be too good to be true were swept away when the painful alternative of continued NATO deterioration was weighed.

Two questions can be fairly asked about the new strategic concept: (1) Will its underlying technology really work as well as claimed? (2) If these claims turn out to be right, will it really make a significant difference in NATO's ability to defend itself?

22

Before addressing the first question, a point of wonderment is raised. General Rogers stated recently, with respect to the new technology: "We do need some increase in numbers of forces to offset Soviet military growth, but far more important to success is the enhancement of our ability to do better with our forces in being and to carry out the essential modernization of these forces."[2] A contradiction seems to be at hand here.

If modernizing the force by exploiting technology is "far more important to success" than increasing the size of the force, why would one not wish to exploit even further the new technology and at the same time reduce the force size? The cost of providing NATO's troops (especially U.S. troops) is much greater than the cost of providing new high-technology weapons. So why not add many more new weapons to a substantially smaller force; that ought to have great appeal to Americans and Europeans increasingly concerned over high defense budgets. If certain advanced conventional weapons can be almost as effective as nuclear weapons (and it long has been agreed that emphasizing nuclear weapons could permit a much smaller defense budget), why should NATO not increase their numbers to the fullest and thereby be able to field a substantially smaller force? Or is it possible that those U.S. military experts who so enthusiastically espouse the new technology either have secret doubts or are unenthusiastic about reducing the size of the U.S. military? No U.S. military organization has ever been enthusiastic about shrinking its size, and certainly would not propose to do so at a time when the administration was doing everything to increase it.

If one peruses with a critical eye the very extensive literature proclaiming the effectiveness of the advanced technology underlying NATO's new conventional doctrine, he is struck by a general omission of what countermeasures the Soviets might take to negate this effectiveness. Surely one would not expect the Soviets to observe this barrage of claims and yet do nothing toward devising measures that might negate the new U.S. conventional doctrine and strategy.

Perhaps the simplest way to thwart the detection and location of targets by radar is to deploy large numbers of cheap decoys that cannot be differentiated from the targets themselves. In this respect, what is to prevent the Soviets from producing tens of thousands of small cheap vehicles (far, far cheaper than tanks and armored personnel carriers) having radar reflectors that would give the same signal to the airborne radars as would the armored vehicles? These vehicles could move forward along with the armor formations, but in different locations, perhaps hopelessly to confuse NATO's target-acquisition abilities. Not being able to locate reliably the real armored targets, the defending NATO forces now would have the almost insuperable problem of having to attack seemingly vastly larger numbers of enemy armored units than they had bargained for. Since these new conventional munitions will be far from cheap, being comparable in price to tactical nuclear weapons, the defensive requirements could be costed out of sight by these cheap decoys. Add to this the substantial probability, based on test experience so far with these new munitions, that a considerable fraction of them won't even work, because of their complexity, and the overall defensive requirements become even more remote.

Even were a means devised to enable distinguishing between tanks and radar decoys, another class of decoys could be devised to confuse the heat-seeking guidance equipment in the submunitions. (We might recall the almost nightly spectacle on TV news during the Lebanese war of Israeli air attacks against the PLO in West Beirut, where the Israeli jets released flares as they came in to drop their bombs. This was done to draw PLO defensive fire, which included small heat-seeking antiaircraft missiles, away from the jets. This tactic succeeded so well that not one Israeli jet was lost.) There is no reason why, like the Israeli jets, Soviet armored vehicles could not dispense heat decoys at the time they come under attack, at but a few yards away, to draw away the submunitions. To kill a tank these submunitions must hit it; a near miss is as good as a mile.

For these reasons, the Soviets may not remain passive to the U.S. propagandizing these new conventional-weapon capabilities and may develop means to reduce sharply their effectiveness. Undoubtedly they will, as they have been doing all along, but there may be other means to defeat NATO, means that they have had in mind all along—nuclear means.

As the Defense Department has said: "Warsaw Pact forces are in fact postured and trained for theaterwide nuclear strikes against NATO nuclear and conventional military forces and for follow-on attacks by their armored conventional forces to exploit the nuclear attack and rapidly seize NATO territory." Indeed! Practically all major Warsaw Pact exercises involve the use of nuclear weapons. Were the Soviets to adhere to their basic nuclear doctrine and capitalize on the nuclear training of their troops (why wouldn't

24

they?), to what avail would the U.S. new conventional look be, even were its claimed capabilities to be fully attained? Very little.

In contrast to the Soviets, NATO has done essentially nothing to prepare itself for nuclear warfare. Even were its conventional firepower to approximate the effectiveness of nuclear weapons (a very dubious proposition, as explained above), the disposition of the forces providing that firepower would present a posture highly vulnerable to nuclear attack.

The aircraft doing the second-echelon target surveillance and conducting a large share of the conventional-weapon delivery operations against these targets all fly out of a limited number of fixed bases that would be wiped out by Soviet nuclear attacks. (Aloft, the surveillance aircraft fly at very high altitude where they would be extremely vulnerable to Soviet nuclear air-defense missiles.) The ground forces capable of waging strikes against the rearward enemy forces consist of large, relatively immobile units that can readily be spotted and destroyed by nuclear weapons. And in large measure this vulnerability holds for the rest of NATO's forces. So, were the Soviets to look to nuclear measures to defeat NATO's new conventional posture, there is every reason to expect they would succeed, easily.

Former Secretary of Defense Donald Rumsfield, in his 1976 "Annual Defense Department Report," dwelt on the threat to NATO posed by Soviet theater nuclear doctrine and capabilities: "Observations indicate that a major danger lies in a massive Warsaw Pact advance into Western Europe characterized by surprise, shock, and rapid air and ground exploitation." Were this danger to materialize one day in the form of a surprise nuclear attack on a NATO force that had achieved its heralded new conventional posture, this achievement would have gone for naught.

Is there any reason to believe that the Soviets would not capitalize on the enormous military advantage that goes with first nuclear use? To say nothing of the enormous investment they have made in nuclear weapons. Or would they instead choose to attack with conventional weapons, perhaps setting themselves up for the kill by NATO's new conventional defense? Or, if that proved to be ineffective (and it probably would), to attack by tactical nuclear weapons that can be highly effective against a force that attacks with conventional weapons only? If nothing else, military common sense would dictate the first mode of attack. Why in heaven's name would the Soviets want to reject their well-established nuclear doctrine and enormous arsenal of modernized nuclear weapons and bow to the U.S. judgment that using these weapons would be too dangerous for them? One would think that they had thought through the problem and its potential dangers well before embarking on their nuclear program and concluded otherwise. There is every evidence that they did exactly that.

This was explained very recently in a book (*Inside the Soviet Army*) by Viktor Suvorov, a pseudonym for a Red Army officer who defected to the West and is now under sentence of death in the USSR. As Suvorov, revealing the brutal (but militarily rational) mentality of Red Army planners, put it:

> The philosophy of the Soviet General Staff is. . . . "If you want to stay alive, kill your enemy. The quicker you finish him off, the less chance he will have to use his own gun." In essence, this is the whole theoretical basis on which their plans for a third world war have been drawn up. The theory is known unofficially in the General Staff as the "axe theory." It is stupid, say the Soviet generals, to start a fistfight if your opponent may use a knife. It is just as stupid to attack him with a knife if he may use an axe. The more terrible the weapon which your opponent may use, the more decisively you must attack him, and the more quickly you must finish him off. Any delay or hesitation in doing this will just give him a fresh opportunity to use his axe on you. To put it briefly, you can only prevent your enemy from using his axe if you use your own first.
>
> The "axe theory" was put forward in all Soviet manuals and handbooks to be read at regimental level and higher. In each of these one of the main sections was headed "Evading the Blow." These handbooks advocated, most insistently, the delivery of a massive preemptive attack on the enemy, as the best method of self-protection. This recommendation was not confined to secret manuals—nonconfidential military publications carried it as well.
>
> In addition to such elementary military logic, there are political and economic reasons which would quite simply compel the Soviet command to make use of the overwhelming proportion of its nuclear armory within the first few minutes of a war.

This is what we have been up against in our efforts, along with NATO, to keep the Red Army from overrunning Europe: namely, a nuclear power that never has had any compunctions about the full unrestrained use of such power. This is in the starkest contrast to ourselves, who have regarded nuclear weapons as unusable and their use as having no value. ("The only value in possessing nuclear weapons is to make sure they can't be used—ever"—President Reagan, November 11, 1983.) And this is going to lead us down the road to disaster if we continue to ignore the nuclear facts of life and go on deceiving ourselves into believing, via conventional-weapon gimmickry and an ostrichlike blindness to Soviet nuclear realities, that somehow we can measure up to and successfully fight the Red Army.

The United States' crucial problem has been that it has chosen to opt out of the nuclear age, whereas the Soviets have unhesitatingly accepted it. We have not been willing seriously to contemplate nuclear weapons as war-fighting instruments; the Soviets always have. This fundamental doctrinal disparity has placed NATO in an untenable position. If we truly desire to have NATO survive, we will have to change our views and accept nuclear weapons as weapons and convince Europe to do the same; but the essential dilemma has been that Europeans believe they can't survive by accepting nuclear weapons.

So long as this dichotomy persists, there is no way for NATO to come up with a realistic conventional defense, or for the U.S. to provide a realistic nuclear defense. And perhaps the most dangerously unrealistic thing we can do for our own security is to concoct new conventional-weapon panaceas to calm down the increasing political discontent over NATO. If Europe seriously wishes to defend itself, it will have to look inward to itself and attempt to resolve its nuclear dilemma, instead of reaching for new U.S. conventional looks that ignore the nuclear realities. This can only be self-deception; it certainly is not fooling the Soviets.

And this is not the full story of our self-deceptive practices, for there are other classes of weapons the Red Army has embraced and incorporated into its strategy and forces: chemical and biological weapons. While the U.S. has for decades been sitting on its hands in this weapon area—the U.S. very recently even rejected the production of advanced chemical weapons (long ago having renounced biological weapons and signed a treaty with the Soviets to this effect, which the Soviets since have flagrantly violated)—the Soviets have single-mindedly moved forward. Today, Red Army combat forces are fully equipped with these weapons and protective measures against potential use by enemy forces. It has been estimated that perhaps as many as a hundred thousand Red Army personnel are assigned to chemical-warfare duties, compared with about two thousand in the U.S. Army. Moreover, the employment of such weapons logically accords with Soviet political objectives for waging ground war—namely, to win the war while sparing the urban-industrial fabric of the defeated country so that it can be exploited after the war to the advantage of the USSR.

When one considers that modern chemical and biological weapons can have levels of effectiveness on the battlefield comparable to tactical nuclear weapons, what conceivable reasons would the Soviets have to refrain from using such weapons in a war with NATO? Probably none whatsoever, for the same reasons they would not refrain from nuclear use. In fact, we should keep in mind that the Soviets already have employed chemical weapons in Afghanistan, and have supplied biological weapons to their Vietnamese surrogates, who have used them (the "yellow-rain" weapons) in Cambodia. If they have had no qualms about using these weapons in wars of such small stakes, why would they not use them in Europe, where the stakes could not be higher? And if they did use them there, with our forces being almost totally unprepared to cope with such attacks, we could lose the war almost as quickly as if they had used nuclear weapons.

This is the mess we have got ourselves into in NATO, because of our unrealistic attitude toward nuclear weapons and our refusal to accept the realities of Soviet nuclear strategy and weapons. We cannot fight the Red Army in Europe and there are no signs that we are about to come to our senses and develop a nuclear strategy and its requisite weapon capabilities (that would have to include the neutron bomb, I might say) that would provide a credible defense. If this situation is to prevail, in all probability there will come a day when something happens, either by Soviet design or by accident (which has been the case before), to touch off a war in which our strategic pledges to our NATO allies are implemented; and this could touch off a nuclear war with the results of *The Day After*. This has to be a totally unacceptable situation for Americans.

Not only can't we fight the Red Army in Europe, but our policies, if a fight occurs, are to conduct nuclear attacks against the Soviet Union itself if all other measures have failed (and they will fail) and the Red Army is overrunning Europe. This would bring about a nuclear war with Russia that we also can't fight. It thus would bring about our defeat; the loss of our freedom; and, in our current position of nakedness to nuclear attack, an appalling loss of U.S. lives and property. Again, this has to be totally unacceptable to the American people, who should demand that we withdraw our nuclear pledges and our military forces from NATO and redirect our commitments to our survival, instead of to our suicide. As for the defense of Europe, this has to be for Europeans to decide; and if they decide to defend themselves realistically—which means a *nuclear* defense—we should help them to the utmost, while we apply

28

ourselves to the utmost to achieve for ourselves a defense against nuclear attack, which is perfectly feasible, as I shall discuss later.

We are now witnessing an attack on our nuclear policies for NATO by a number of former key U.S. officials (including Robert Strange McNamara, secretary of defense under Presidents Kennedy and Johnson) who were mainly responsible for the policies in the first place, but now deny they really meant them. The essence of these attacks recently has been summed up by McNamara: "It will be recalled that the strategy calls for the [NATO] Alliance to initiate nuclear war with battlefield weapons if conventional defenses fail, and to escalate the type of nuclear weapons used (and therefore the targets of these weapons), as necessary, up to and including the use of strategic forces against targets in the USSR itself. Given the tremendous devastation which these Soviet strategic forces that survived a U.S. first strike would now be able to inflict on this country, it is difficult to imagine any U.S. president, under any circumstances, initiating a strategic strike except in retaliation against a Soviet nuclear strike."*[3]

If McNamara is right on this issue—we should pray that he is and that no U.S. president would risk the suicide of his country in behalf of allies who already have lost their battle—then in what position are some two hundred thousand U.S. combat troops in Europe? The answer is simple: they are in the position of being hostage to the Red Army, which can defeat them and send the survivors off to slave-labor camps (where hundreds of thousands of Germans went in World War II)—with impunity, for we would have no rational recourse for saving them; committing suicide for them is hardly rational.

During World War I, before we entered the war, when the U.S. held to its longstanding (since it was born) refusal to get entangled in European wars (which George Washington, in his Farewell Address, had warned against), an extremely popular song with American mothers was "I Didn't Raise My Boy to Be a Soldier." Today, for the reasons given above, American mothers rightly could sing "I Didn't Raise My Boy to Be a Hostage," which is the status of their sons in Europe. Still again, this has to be intolerable to the American people, whose leadership so far has not told them the true story of what our situation in NATO really is.

---

* Remarks very similar, if less impassioned, to those of Henry Kissinger a few years ago: "The European allies should not keep asking us to multiply strategic assurances that we cannot possibly mean, or if we do mean, we should not want to execute because if we execute we risk the destruction of civilization." (Speech: "NATO—The Next Thirty Years," Brussels, Belgium, Sept. 1, 1979.)

If one confronts U.S. officials over the mess I've described and with the inconsistency and self-contradiction of U.S. policy statements on NATO, in which they largely ignore their own facts, the usual answer goes something like this: "Well, what you say may be true but you have to keep in mind that our policy, despite all its twists and turns, still succeeds in deterring the Red Army from attacking Europe. For all its faults, our NATO policy, with its serious military deficiencies, obviously must cause enough uncertainty in the minds of Red Army planners to keep them from attacking. So why not stick with a good thing until a better one comes along." This has about the same ring of conviction as the "peace in our time" assurances of Neville Chamberlain on the eve of World War II must have had for Winston Churchill.

For so vital an issue, the fate of Europe and perhaps our own country as well, to peg our survival on something so intangible as sowing uncertainty in the Soviet mind, which we never have really understood, seems at a minimum to be wildly wishful thinking. There is no way for our planners to decide how the Soviets gauge this uncertainty in deciding whether or not to go to war. Nor does this factor have very much to do in preventing the Soviets from being drawn into a progression of human events such as the escalatory ladder scenario in *The Day After*, wherein they strike first against the U.S. for fear that we may get the jump on them. These are the real-world possibilities that bear little relationship to whether or not the Soviet cause of action will be seriously swayed by considerations about U.S. willingness to implement a policy whose baseline is the threat of U.S. suicide and unacceptable devastation to the USSR, and a virtual certainty that Europe will fall into the hands of the Red Army while this is going on. Such a threat by the U.S. not only has to be incredible; it has to be insane. Do we want to risk our future by holding forth our insanity to the Russians to scare them off? That is not too comforting a thought, but that is in effect what we're doing right now. This should be intolerable to Americans.

Very likely, the Soviets have regarded us as irrational and even insane. That would go a long way to explain why they have been building up their defensive, as well as their offensive, forces at such a clip—to survive, just in case a nuclear war breaks out, which the Soviets long have regarded as quite likely. At least half the Soviet budget allocated to nuclear war is spent for the direct defense of the USSR—in sharp contrast to the U.S. budget, which is almost entirely spent on offensive weapons. Going on the premise that the Soviets are in a far better position to assess the effectiveness of their defensive capabilities than we are, who is to say that their sanity in wanting to stay alive and survive as a nation hasn't allowed them to make hard rational calculations to convince themselves that they can deal with the threat implied by our insane policy? Again, it is not very comforting to have the future of our country depend so heavily on such a threat, when the threat of war itself looms so distinctly, as brought out in *The Day After*.

The Soviets never have dismissed the threat of war from their minds. Their leaders have always been historically conscious of war and its recurrence and have warned of the necessity to prepare for it. Lenin regarded peace as little more than a respite between wars. In 1974 Leonid Brezhnev admonished, "It would be extremely dangerous if the opinion became firmly established in public circles that everything is now completely in order and that the threat of war has become illusory." The following year his defense minister, Andrei Grechko, repeated the warning: "The danger of war remains a grim reality of our times." In other words, the U.S. hope that somehow the uncertainties associated with our nuclear deterrence policies will dissuade the Soviets from thinking about and planning for war may have been little more than wishful thinking. There is no hard evidence that the Soviets place any faith in the workability of deterrence, as we do. For them, the eventuality of nuclear war is real indeed.

As of now, the greatest danger of our getting into a war with the Russians is in the Middle East, a war occasioned by our intervention in still another Arab-Israeli war. To place this danger in proper perspective, we might go back a decade and consider what almost happened in one of these wars, the Yom Kippur war of 1973. That war, and the events that accompanied it, probably came closer to producing a U.S.–USSR military confrontation and a potential of nuclear war than any other event to date, including the Cuban "missile crisis" of 1962. In contemplating its future role in the Middle East, the United States should take stock of what happened in 1973, and what has happened since to the U.S.–USSR military balance in this area and its relationship to the wisdom of U.S. military intervention.

On 6 October 1973 the Yom Kippur war began with a surprise attack against Israel by Egypt and Syria. After initial successes, the Arab armies were repulsed and two weeks later Israeli forces were deep in Arab territory. The United Nations succeeded in arranging for a ceasefire, which managed to hold on the Syrian front but fell apart in Egypt, where Israeli forces had trapped the Egyptian Third Army and fighting continued. The Third Army was in danger of being destroyed, which would have been a great disaster for Egypt—a disaster that neither the United States nor the Soviet Union desired. Such a disaster to Egypt, the United States believed, would work against establishing a durable peace in the Middle East and weaken the U.S. position in that region. The Soviets desired no disaster because they were on the Arab side, having armed and trained the Egyptian and Syrian forces.

Having a common objective for a change, the United States and Russia got together and agreed to seek an enforcement of the fractured ceasefire. The United States placed great pressure on Israel to forgo the destruction of the encircled Egyptian forces but failed in its efforts to stop the fighting. As a consequence, the Soviets, feeling that they had been betrayed by the United States, began to prepare for military intervention.

All the Soviet airborne troops were placed on alert. Amphibious assault vessels and helicopter carriers were moved into the Mediterranean. And there was ample evidence that the Soviets had transported nuclear warheads for a brigade of missiles near Cairo which could have reached deep into Israeli territory. An ominous situation had developed.

The United States reacted by placing its military forces on a higher level of alert. Several dozen B-52 strategic nuclear bombers were shifted from their bases in Guam to the United States. A super carrier, the *John F. Kennedy,* was dispatched toward the Mediterranean. The Thirty-second Airborne Division was readied for dispatch. All of this was intended to show the Soviets that the United States was readying itself for a potential confrontation with the Russians, a confrontation holding the risk of nuclear war.

Finally, the Israelis pulled away from the fighting and the war ended. But a hair-raising crisis had existed that held the threat of escalating to Armageddon for all involved. As to whether the United States or the Soviet Union would have backed down had Israel refused to stop the war, we'll never know.

One thing is clear, however. Had the United States, to save Israel, joined the escalatory process to the top rung of the ladder (thermonuclear war with the USSR), that would have been insane: America would have succeeded in committing suicide; Israel would have perished under Soviet nuclear attack; and, to one extent or another, the world would have suffered from the effects of general nuclear war. Speaking as an American, I hope this is one risk my country, the United States, will never again take in behalf of Israel, or any other ally, for that matter.

The trouble is, though, that current U.S. policy toward Israel does not preclude a similar crisis from happening should still another war break out. Which strongly suggests that in providing Israel with military assistance, the United States should seek to guarantee that another Yom Kippur war crisis, involving the threat of Soviet intervention, never again can arise. This can be accomplished by U.S. insistence that Israel change its military doctrine to achieve a defense-oriented capability. Indeed, as a consequence of the Lebanese war, the attitude of the American people toward Israel's military doctrine has changed sharply from that of past years. A June 1982 Gallup poll asked the following questions and received the following response:

> Some people say the U.S. should require that all weapons sent by the U.S. to Israel should be used only for defensive purposes. Other people say that Israel should be able to use these weapons in any way they feel is necessary. Which point of view comes closer to your own?

Israel's Use of U.S. Weapons
(Based on aware group)

Defensive use only 64%
Any way necessary 26%
No opinion 10%

The Yom Kippur war, and the peril it posed to American security, occurred more than ten years ago. At that time the United States probably held a significant edge in theater nuclear firepower that could be applied to the region, and a state of parity was declared to exist between U.S. and Soviet strategic nuclear forces. This is not to say that it would have made sense for the United States to attempt to exploit a perceived advantage in local nuclear capabilities by initiating the use of nuclear weapons, had a military confrontation with the Soviets occurred. Rather, it is to say that the Soviets ostensibly, having an inferior theater nuclear capability, might have refrained from nuclear use and sought to resolve the conflict by conventional warfare. But we're speculating on what might have happened a decade back. Times have changed since then and a drastically different nuclear situation exists today.

Since 1973, U.S. theater nuclear capabilities relevant to another

Israeli-Arab war have not changed in any appreciable way. On the other hand, Soviet capabilities have increased hugely, to an extent where they are far superior to those of the United States. They now pose a military threat of a far greater magnitude than was the case in 1973.

Soviet naval nuclear capabilities in the Mediterranean have greatly expanded. Firing nuclear-tipped missiles from surface ships and submarines, the Soviets, in a surprise attack against the U.S. Sixth Fleet, could easily do away with the bulk of the U.S. surface-ship capabilities—which would be sitting ducks to nuclear missile attack.

Based in the Soviet Union are increasing numbers, already in the many hundreds, of modern supersonic Backfire nuclear bombers and theater ballistic nuclear missiles, which have full coverage over the entire Middle East and Mediterranean areas, to back up the Red Army should it be necessary in this arena. The United States has no such capabilities.

In the strategic nuclear area, since the Yom Kippur war the Soviet Union has forged ahead of the United States to gain what President Reagan has described as "a definite margin of superiority." Under these conditions, for the United States to risk nuclear war by risking a confrontation with the Soviets in the Middle East would defy sanity. The strategic nuclear balance in 1973 may have had the United States believing that nuclear parity would deter Soviet nuclear action and that the Soviets would back down short of the brink. Today, however, with the balance in the Soviet's favor, increasingly so, they would have little reason to be the first to back down in another Mideast confrontation.

This unhappy fact of life excludes, assuming any sanity remains in our country, the possibility of U.S. military intervention in the event of another Mideast war. Should Israel once again position itself so that its military forces threaten the integrity of an Arab country, and should the USSR threaten to come to the aid of that country, Israel would have to go it alone. In view of the overwhelming military force the Soviets could bring to bear, that would place Israel in an untenable position, whether or not it used nuclear weapons. The real threat to Israel in the future, if it continues with its past military doctrine, will be the Soviet Union, not the Arab nations, however powerfully they may arm themselves with conventional weapons. And this compels Israel to change its doctrine in favor of a guaranteed defense of its borders to ensure that they will never be placed in this position. It also should compel the U.S.

34

to pressure the Israelis to effect such a change, for the sake of both countries. To accomplish this, we should help them to the fullest.

In this respect, the new "strategic-cooperation" program the U.S. established with Israel in 1982 is operating against the security of both countries. It does not provide Israel with the means to deal realistically with the Soviet Union in the event of another Arab-Israeli war, which seems more likely with each passing day; and it does enhance the probability of U.S. intervention in another war and a U.S. confrontation with the Soviet Union.

We have already discussed the utter futility, irrationality, and danger of the U.S. intervening in the Persian Gulf to prevent the Russians from choking off the flow of oil. If we add to this the danger of our intervening in Arab-Israeli wars, the message becomes very clear: we can't fight the Red Army in the Middle East. We should let the nations that get into such wars decide for themselves either how to settle them or, far better, how to avoid them.

In the Far East, the major danger of a U.S.–USSR confrontation arises from the increasing possibility of another war in Korea. Three decades ago President Eisenhower was able to bring the Korean war to an end by threatening the use of nuclear weapons; with our enormous nuclear superiority, the threat worked. Today the Soviets possess a far larger and more capable arsenal of nuclear weapons in the Far East than we have. Were they to intervene in behalf of their North Korean ally and employ these weapons against U.S. forces, the latter, fighting in behalf of South Korea, would be demolished. In this event, what would we do? Begin a nuclear exchange with the USSR? For heaven's sake, no!

The survival of South Korea may mean a great deal to us, but our own survival has to be paramount to us. We will least ensure this by dispatching U.S. forces to fight there. As was briefly our policy for helping Asian allies after the Vietnam debacle—the so-called Nixon doctrine; praised by most Americans then but apparently forgotten by most Americans now—we should do everything we can to enable South Korea to defend itself, except send American forces to fight there. The dangers of doing that have become far too great. Whatever the price may be for enabling South Korea to defend itself fades into insignificance compared to the price we may pay if we get into a war with Russia by fighting there once again.

We cannot fight the Red Army. Had we been realistic, many years ago, about employing nuclear weapons in ground warfare, we could have put ourselves and our allies in a position where we could have presented the Soviets with a realistic ground defense. That, however, is water long, long over the dam; and today there are no signs that we desire to correct the situation, nor would our NATO allies allow us to. As a result, we have got ourselves into an extremely dangerous mess over our policy of trying to contain the Red Army, and because of our self-imposed shackles, we can do precious little about it.

One of Murphy's laws is Thompson's rule: "If you can't do anything about it, don't." If we can't do anything about the Red Army, let's stop pretending we can. Short of trying to bluff the Russians with the threat of strategic nuclear war, we can do nothing; and if the Russians were to call our bluff some day, as happened in *The Day After*, we would be in a nuclear war that we could only lose—for we certainly can't fight a strategic nuclear war with Russia.

3

Can We Fight a Strategic Nuclear War with Russia?

> It is quite another question to know the truth. There is an assertion that the CIA shall be in position to know the truth and be able to communicate it to us. From a military point of view, such would be considered an ultimate requirement. The truth is the reality of events. Now, how do you get it? You go out and look for information, which you hope is relevant or in some way related. But that is not always the case. A lot of information is misinformation. This is particularly so when we are trying to get information from a closed society that realizes information that we think is of interest to our security is absolutely vital to theirs, and every effort is made to deny us access to it. They can also grudgingly release information to us that we later find out frequently to be misinformation.
>
> Dr. John S. Foster, Jr.
> Member, President Reagan's Foreign
> Intelligence Advisory Board

IN THE EARLY 1950s, before "national technical means" (NTM) of intelligence (that is, peripheral radar stations, U-2 airplanes, and reconnaissance satellites) were developed that allowed us to look out at and down upon the Soviet Union to see what appeared to be going on at the surface, our assessment of Russian strategic nuclear capabilities was little more than a guessing game. Under such conditions, our nuclear intelligence was bound to become highly politicized: military services more or less conjured up estimates that would best further their parochial interests, and administrations tailored intelligence estimates to further their political interests, which always involved the next election. Even within a given military service, this process went on as advocates of one nuclear-weapon system vied with those of another.

Although such fun and games certainly did not work to gain the most effective U.S. nuclear-weapons arsenal to fight a war, since during this period we were unquestionably far ahead of the Russians, in the short run our national security was not being critically affected. And besides, in those days of our "massive-retaliation" strategic nuclear doctrine, according to which most of our bombs were directed toward known targets—for example, urban-industrial facilities—it really didn't matter all that much that we might not be able to find and destroy Soviet military nuclear targets, in fighting and winning a war. As Gen. Curtis LeMay, boss of the U.S. Strategic Air Command (which then owned all the strategic nuclear weapons), explained his philosophy of war with Russia to me, "When we kill enough of them [Russians], they'll stop fighting."

Today, however, a drastically different equation exists. We no longer enjoy a huge nuclear superiority; in fact, it is generally accepted that the Soviets now have an overall nuclear advantage, a view shared by President Reagan. We have discarded our urban-industrial attack strategies of the past and now base our nuclear strategy mainly on the ability to destroy a wide range of military targets in the USSR. As Secretary of Defense Caspar Weinberger has said: "We disagree with those who hold that deterrence should be based on nuclear weapons designed to destroy cities rather than military targets. Deliberately designing weapons aimed at populations is neither necessary nor sufficient for deterrence."[1]

At first glance, one would find it difficult, at least for moral reasons, to disagree with Weinberger's remarks. Surely, one would prefer a nuclear strategy and attendant weapon design requirements that are based on the desire to attack the Russian nuclear-weapon capabilities, in order to lessen the damage they can inflict upon us. This certainly is morally preferable to a strategy aimed at enemy civilians who can do nothing to hurt us directly and whose destruction might prompt retaliation leading to the destruction of our own civilian population. As Weinberger has stated, "If we are forced to retaliate and can only respond by destroying population centers, we invite the destruction of our own population." Unfortunately, if one probes the real meaning of John Foster's remarks, a distinct possibility exists that either we may be forced to go back to targeting Soviet cities or we may capitulate to a Soviet nuclear attack—unless we make drastic changes in our nuclear strategy and nuclear-weapon requirements.

Certain elements of the Soviet strategic nuclear-weapons program have been very puzzling. For example:

• Why have the Soviets gone through five generations of ICBM development since the beginning of their program, with at least three new model weapons supposedly now in the force, while the United States has gone through but two generations with only one not-so-new model surviving—the Minuteman missile?

• Why have the Soviets allegedly deployed all of their ICBMs in silos, whose locations are known to us, or in the vicinity of those silos where they could be reloaded after a first launch had taken place, and where they may become vulnerable to U.S. nuclear attack?

• Why have the Soviets supposedly agreed (in the SALT II arms-control treaty) to a U.S. request to forgo the deployment of the highly survivable SS-16 mobile ICBMs that they have developed and tested?

• Why have the Soviets allegedly refrained from producing and deploying a new intercontinental strategic bomber, while the United States has embarked upon the B-1 program?

• Why have the Soviets, for more than twenty years, allowed us to send reconnaissance satellites over their territory supposedly to ferret out vital information about their strategic nuclear capabilities?

For many years we have orbited highly sophisticated satellites over and positioned radars in countries adjoining the USSR to determine the kinds of strategic nuclear weapons they have developed, produced, and deployed. From these sensor systems we have gained physical information that (we say) has allowed us to assess the nature and performance of these weapons: how many weapon launchers and what kind are being deployed, and where; and to what military purpose these weapons are directed. How unrealistic has this assessment been?

39

As a case in point, consider the bewildering diversity of ICBMs the Soviets have developed and (we maintain) installed in some fourteen hundred hardened silos. This missile force, determined by NTM, presently consists of five different weapons—the SS-11, -13, -17, -18, and -19—and contains thirteen different models. The SS-11s and SS-13s are of relatively ancient vintage, having been first deployed seventeen and fifteen years ago, respectively. The SS-17s, SS-18s, and SS-19s began to enter the force in 1975.

Using NTM techniques, we supposedly have been able to determine the size of these missiles, the silos where they are housed, and their performance.*

Needless to say, such data have been judged of great value to the United States: enabling us to assign nuclear weapons to attack these critical targets and to detect their launching in an attack on us. Yet, is it not curious that the Soviets have perhaps given us information that we could use to the great detriment of their security should a nuclear war occur? This neither accords with the habits of how nations usually operate to protect their vital security nor represents common military sense. Unless there were no practical alternatives to building and basing such missiles, why should the Soviets have been so benevolent toward us? Perhaps they haven't.

It is one thing for the Soviets to have conducted such a huge and diverse program of developing and testing their ICBMs. It is quite another thing, however, for them to decide on how many of what kind to produce and where to deploy them. Keep in mind that the SALT agreements on offensive arms limitations, as applied to ICBMs, placed no constraints on the numbers and kinds of missiles that could be produced. SALT fixed only the numbers and kinds of fixed launchers (that we assume are silos) that could be constructed. Which brings up a basic question.

Have the Soviets embarked on their massive silo construction program; allowed us to "see" missiles being loaded into silos; conducted "operational" flight tests from these silos and reloading exercises—all for the purpose of deceiving us into believing they actually have a silo-based force of ICBMs—while, at the same time, deploying a concealed force of missiles of a much different size

---

* Based on this determination, the Pentagon has claimed that the breakdown of missiles in silos is 550 SS-11s, 60 SS-13s, 150 SS-17s, 308 SS-18s, and 330 SS-19s. As for the Soviet rationale behind this breakdown, we have no sound idea, although this is in part a product of the SALT I and II agreements on how many of what-sized silos could be constructed.

and composition elsewhere, which could not be targeted by U.S. nuclear weapons and, thus, would be invulnerable to attack? Moreover, have the Soviets used the strategic arms-control process, via SALT agreements, to constrain U.S. strategic nuclear deployments by misleading the United States into believing that the USSR was similarly constraining its own deployments—while the United States blissfully believed it was verifying the agreements by NTM?

In general, the cost of developing a major new strategic nuclear weapon is but a small fraction of producing and operating it. On this basis, a plausible explanation can be made as to why the Soviets, over the years, have *developed* so many new ICBMs, having so many different models, but may *not* have elected to produce and deploy all of them. This also can help explain why a distinct probability exists that the Soviets, as part of a massive strategic disinformation policy, may have given the United States the impression—gained through NTM—that their ICBM deployment is principally, if not even totally, in some fourteen hundred silos whose construction has been so easy for us to observe, and whose missile operations (including occasional flight testing) we have so easily been able to monitor.

During the mid-1970s, when the United States openly revealed its shift in strategic doctrine away from assured destruction and toward a capability to go after military targets, the Soviets must have realized that their ICBMs were becoming prime candidates for U.S. nuclear targeting. By signing the SALT I offensive arms limitation agreement a few years earlier, which seemingly had cast the ICBM balance as to the number of silos (fixed launchers), the Soviets, it would have appeared, had cast themselves into a position of increasing ICBM vulnerability, as U.S. attack capabilities increased. Not only were they becoming vulnerable to a possible first strike (resulting from the U.S. strategic nuclear commitment to its NATO allies), but their ability to employ ICBMs over an extended period after the war began was in jeopardy. (Having a survivable intrawar strategic nuclear capability has long been a high-priority Soviet requirement.)

Based on military common sense alone, a Soviet decision to go on installing its missiles in silos and developing reload capabilities for subsequent silo launches, in the face of our increasing attack capabilities, would have been highly questionable. Perhaps, then, the Soviets never made such a decision, but chose instead to mislead us, through deceiving our NTM into believing that they did, while deploying certain of their new-generation missiles elsewhere. By *certain* of their new missiles (SS-17s, -18s, and -19s, which were developed in the early 1970s), what is implied here is that the Soviets may never have had it in mind to deploy all of them, with each of their different models. Rather, they may have decided to deploy away from silo fields only those missiles that best enhanced their military capabilities, and have given the impression to U.S. NTM that they were emplacing all their missiles in silos.

As an example of this possibility, take the SS-18, by far the largest Soviet ICBM, which has been tested with ten or more warheads. This missile has been singled out by the United States as the most serious first-strike threat to the survivability of Minuteman, being able to launch more than three thousand warheads from 308 silos. Yet, like our MX ICBM, which will carry ten warheads, from a vulnerability standpoint the SS-18 does not seem like a good bargain, with such a high concentration of vulnerable firepower. In this sense, might not the Soviets have chosen seemingly to deploy the SS-18 for our NTM to "see," for the political purpose of advertising their nuclear strength, while actually deploying smaller missiles elsewhere that more readily could be concealed from U.S. NTM?

As mentioned, the cost of developing ICBMs is small compared with that of producing and operating them. Moreover, the cost of constructing hardened silos is but a fraction of the missile development and production cost and does not constitute a serious price of deception. As such, deceiving us into believing that a large force of SS-18s is being deployed in silos could reap substantial political benefits, as to our perception of the threat; and even greater military benefits—having a hidden invulnerable ICBM capability, perhaps consisting of smaller, more concealable missiles, well in excess of that we ascribe to SS-18s in silos.

One should realize that such deployment, while certainly against the spirit of the SALT agreements, would not directly violate them. These arrangements dealt only with ICBMs operating from fixed launchers, interpreted by the United States to mean *silos*. In this sense, since Soviet ICBMs can be and are fired from their containing canisters, which need not be fixed in place, concealed deployment of these weapons would not constitute a SALT violation. In fact, this very point was made by Caspar Weinberger in attempting to defend the MX Dense Pack deployment; silos, he argued, did not necessarily represent fixed launchers for this missile system, and thus Dense Pack was not constrained by SALT.

42

That the United States would regard such deception by the Soviets as a dastardly deed, were it to be uncovered, goes without saying; but we could not directly accuse them of a flagrant treaty violation. Moreover, considering the enormity of such a Soviet deed and its consequences for U.S. survival, it is not even clear that the U.S. government would want to bring this out into the open—for fear of the domestic political consequences—or even admit it to itself. Rather it might decide to ignore the Soviet perfidy and subtly shift back to a strategic policy of assured destruction, hoping, perhaps desperately, that, as formerly was claimed, it represented the best way to deter nuclear war. And, for domestic political reasons, continue with strategic arms control negotiations.

In the early 1970s the Soviets completed development of the SS-16 mobile ICBM; a single-warhead missile using solid fuel, which considerably enhances mobility. A few years later, in SALT II, they agreed to a U.S. protocol to cease production and testing of this missile, and not to deploy it; although they were not legally bound by the treaty itself so to constrain themselves. In 1982 it was reported that perhaps between one hundred and two hundred SS-16 launchers had been deployed (under cover) at the Plesetsk missile testing center in Siberia. The director of the U.S. Arms Control and Disarmament Agency stated his concern over this possibility: "Certainly evidence has come along that causes great concern about whether the SS-16 provisions of SALT II are being respected." However, this episode was short-lived and at this juncture, as has been the case for other Soviet arms-control infractions, the matter has been swept under the carpet.

When one considers the high survivability of mobile missiles—especially in the USSR, where they can operate over such a huge expanse with their location essentially unknown to us, allowing nuclear strikes to be made against us during an extended nuclear war—why would the Soviets have been willing to forgo SS-16 deployment in SALT II? Why would they have forgone the chance to get a big jump on us, especially since we had neither developed such a capability nor expressed any interest in such a development? (It was but two years ago that the U.S. decided to develop a mobile ICBM, the Midgetman missile whose deployment will not take place until the 1990s.) Why would they give up a valuable missile system on their side, when we had nothing of the kind to give up on our side? The Soviets are not known for a propensity to practice unilateral disarmament. And maybe they haven't, in their mobile missile program.

A few years after the SS-16 development program ended, the Soviets began to deploy the SS-20 intermediate-range ballistic missile. The deployment caused such consternation in NATO that, in 1979, requirements were established for Pershing II and ground-launched cruise missiles to counter the SS-20 threat. And this has resulted in even more consternation, as European countries have been deeply split over the deployment of these missiles. At present, close to four hundred SS-20 launchers are believed to have been deployed in the USSR.

The SS-20 is very like the SS-16, being solid-fueled and able to use the same launcher. In two departments, however, the SS-20 represents a considerable technological advance over the SS-16: it is MIRVed, carrying three warheads, and is far more accurate. Based on our NTM observations of SS-20 flight tests, we have assigned a range of 5,000 kilometers (3,000 miles) to this missile, placing it in the intermediate-range category, but even then falling only 10 percent short of our definition of ICBM range.

It cannot be stressed too strongly how limited our understanding is of the SS-20. Not being constrained by any arms-control agreement for intermediate-range nuclear missiles, as have their strategic weapons, the Soviets have been free to conduct their SS-20 program as they have seen fit. However, they also have seen fit to place a veil of secrecy over this program; this has resulted in extensive efforts by them to deny U.S. NTM the ability fully to monitor SS-20 flight testing. To thwart this ability the Soviets have conducted tests under cover of night and have encoded test telemetry.

Considering our essential ignorance of this missile, because of these Soviet concealment tactics, one might wonder whether our appraisal of the SS-20 has been guided more by Soviet deception and disinformation than by hard facts. Could it be that the SS-20 has all along been a variable-range mobile ICBM development —representing a distinct improvement over the SS-16 and capable of striking targets in both America and Europe—that the Soviets preferred to incorporate into their strategic arsenal? There are sound reasons to believe that this may have been the case.

At the same time the SS-20 was under development a new family of advanced mobile theater nuclear ballistic missiles was also being developed—the SS-21, SS-22, and SS-23—having substantial coverage over critical nuclear targets in Europe. In addition, new ICBMs and supersonic nuclear bombers and fighter bombers were being provided which could be employed against the full range of European targets. This panoply of weapons would provide the

Soviets with full coverage, at high accuracy, over *all* nuclear targets in NATO, with more, far more, than enough warheads to neutralize those targets. In this respect, where did the SS-20 fit into Soviet requirements for modernizing its theater nuclear missiles: especially as to the numbers of those weapons that have been built so far—probably more than a thousand missiles holding thousands of nuclear warheads? Maybe it didn't fit into Soviet plans and was never intended to; for the reasons given above.

If, indeed, the SS-20 was primarily intended to be a mobile ICBM that the Soviets could hold as an invaluable reserve force in an extended nuclear war, then we have been dangerously deceived by the Soviets. We have also been guilty of dangerously deceiving ourselves, and our NATO allies as well, whom we have led to believe that the SS-20 is primarily a threat against Europe. Had we looked more objectively and sensibly at the SS-20 as the Soviets might view it, we might never have started the ill-conceived Pershing II and cruise missile programs and the ill-fated Intermediate-range Nuclear Forces (INF) talks with the Soviets. And avoided the sorry state of affairs in NATO today.

In 1974 the Soviets first deployed their supersonic Backfire bomber, supposedly an aircraft of very limited capability for bombing targets in the United States. Although there was considerable disagreement in the U.S. intelligence community over Backfire performance, the United States accepted, primarily for arms-control reasons, to achieve the SALT II accords, the Soviet claim that Backfire was a medium bomber for use in the Eurasian theater. In this capacity, presumabily it would have diverse roles for nuclear and conventional attack, and antiship and reconnaissance missions. (Backfire, were it to have a midair refueling capability, could have extensive coverage over U.S. targets. However, under the provisions of the SALT agreements, the Soviets have promised not to equip the aircraft with fuel probes to achieve this capability. Presumably, NTM could detect such a violation.)

If one examines the rationale for designing Backfire as a medium bomber, a puzzlement arises, similar to the SS-20 case. The same year that Backfire was introduced, the Fencer nuclear-strike tactical aircraft entered the force. Like Backfire, Fencer was a high-performance airplane. It had a Mach 2 speed, all-weather, low-altitude penetration capability; and a maximum combat radius of about 2,000 kilometers, comparable to that of the U.S. FB-111 fighter bomber that is based in the United Kingdom, and that is capable of conducting nuclear strikes deep into the western part of the Soviet Union. The large range of Fencer permitted nuclear strikes to be made over the entirety of NATO Europe. And this raises the question: How valid a requirement existed for developing Backfire as a theater nuclear weapon system?

When Backfire was introduced, the Soviet strategic bomber force already was becoming obsolescent. This force consisted of two subsonic bombers—Bear and Bison—which were first deployed in 1956. Having made clear, in its doctrinal writings, that aircraft would play an indispensable role in an extended nuclear war, it would have been logical for the Soviets to introduce a new generation of strategic bombers around the time Backfire was first deployed. That may have been precisely what happened.

At the time the Backfire force (now estimated to consist of about two hundred aircraft, twice the number of U.S. B-1 bombers now scheduled for production) was first building up, the United States, concluding that the critical nuclear threat was the Soviet ballistic missile force, had decided to eliminate its continental air defenses, now a fait accompli. If indeed the Soviets have been deploying Backfire primarily to be used against the United States, in view of emasculated U.S. air defenses those aircraft will have a free ride to destroy targets remaining after the Soviet first strike; which cannot be said for U.S. bombers attempting to penetrate massive Soviet air defenses. As for the SS-20, we may have dangerously deceived ourselves, with some help from the Soviets, on the real role of the Backfire bomber and, in the process, further imperiled our security.

Ever since I first found myself in the West, I have been soaking up information of all kinds. I have visited dozens of libraries, seen hundreds of films . . . I keep on and on going to films. One day I went to an excellent one about the burglary of a diamond warehouse. The thieves broke into the enormous building with great skill, put a dozen alarms out of action, opened enormously thick doors and finally reached the secret innermost room in which the safes stood. Of course, in addition to all the transmitters, alarm devices, and so on, there were TV cameras, through which a guard kept constant watch on what was happening in the room where the safes were. But the thieves, too, were ingenious. They had with them a photograph of the room, taken earlier. They put this in front of the cameras and, using it as a screen, emptied the safes. The guards sensed that something was happening. They began to feel vaguely uneasy. But looking at the television screen they were able to convince themselves that everything was quiet in the safe room.

I am sometimes told that the American spy-satellites are keeping a careful watch on what is happening in the Soviet Union. They take infrared photographs of the country from above and from oblique angles, their photographs are compared, electronic, heat and all other emissions are measured, radio transmissions are intercepted and painstakingly analyzed. It is impossible to fool satellites. When I hear this, I always think of the trio of sympathetic villains who hid from the cameras behind a photograph, using it as a shield behind which to fill their bags with diamonds. Incidentally, the film ended happily for the thieves. . . .

The Chief Directorate of Strategic Deception does exactly what the sympathetic trio did—they show the watchful eye of the camera a reassuring picture, behind the shelter of which the gangsters who call themselves the Communist Party of the Soviet Union, the Soviet Army, Military Industry, and so forth, go about their business. . . .

The Chief Directorate differs from our resourceful burglars in presenting false pictures not for a few hours but for decades. It has at its disposal not three crooks but tens of thousands of highly qualified specialists and almost unlimited powers in its dealings with generals, marshals, and those who run the military industries over the concealment of the true state of affairs.

There is no doubt that these activities enable the Politburo, without great difficulty, to empty the pockets of those in the West who will not understand that they are dealing with organized crime, committed by a state which is operating on a worldwide scale.

These remarks are from Viktor Suvorov's book *Inside the Soviet Army*. If they are accurate, they effectively answer the question stated previously: "Why have the Soviets for more than twenty years allowed us to send reconnaissance satellites over their territory to ferret out vital information about their strategic nuclear capabilities?" The answer, based on Suvorov's appraisal, seems plain enough: They haven't. And if they haven't, the United States has been deceived (and deceived itself) into an extremely perilous predicament. For, in our current strategic nuclear posture, we may be virtually unable to fight a nuclear war with Russia in accordance with our declaratory policy. Such a deplorable situation may not succeed in deterring nuclear war in the future.

The shift in U.S. strategic doctrine away from assured destruction (that is, "city busting") and toward military operations (that is, counterforce) was first announced in January 1974 by Defense Secretary James Schlesinger. Should the Soviets make a strategic nuclear attack against us with a restrained counterforce strike, the

47

United States henceforth would have the capability of striking back in a "selective" manner, striking only crucial military targets while avoiding unnecessary damage to urban industrial areas and civilians in those areas.

In summer 1980 the new doctrine was reaffirmed by President Jimmy Carter in the form of Presidential Directive No. 59 (PD-59). In addition to traditional nuclear targets such as ICBMs, nuclear submarine bases, and airfields capable of handling strategic bombers, PD-59 emphasized control targets—military, Communist party, and internal security control—and military forces capable of projecting their power away from their peacetime bases. Defense Secretary Harold Brown explained that this expanded target list was "designed with the Soviets in mind," and would "take account of what we know about Soviet perspectives on these issues, for, by definition, deterrence requires shaping Soviet assessments about the risks of war—assessments they will make using their models, not ours."

However, in comparing the new U.S. nuclear doctrine with that of the Soviets, a critical question emerges: Does the United States really know enough about the Soviet nuclear target system (and about Soviet efforts to deny the United States access to this information, such as target location) to implement realistically and effectively its proclaimed selective targeting strategy? Or, alternatively, is our strategic doctrine little more than mouthed pieties unsupported by military capabilities?

The basic U.S. problem with its strategic planning has been that while we are finally beginning to recognize Soviet doctrine, we have yet to accept some of its most central tenets. One, perhaps the most crucial tenet, is the importance of *surprise* and the need to employ secrecy, cover, and deception to mislead the enemy, to enhance surprise.

Surprise appears to be the single most important principle of nuclear war in Soviet thinking. As stated in their military literature, it is achieved mainly "as a result of poor knowledge by the adversary of one's true intentions, as a result of subjective errors in assessing intentions and plans, as well as a result of shallow analyses of measures taken to achieve surprise." In Soviet military textbooks, dictionaries, and encyclopedias, objectives such as "misleading the enemy about one's intentions" and "leading the enemy into error concerning one's own intentions" always appear atop the list, closely followed by other important concepts such as "covert preparations," "unexpected use of nuclear weapons," "camouflage actions," and "the use of means and methods unknown to the enemy." In other words, *disinformation* is a key element of the Soviets' strategy, to implement their principle of surprise.

In a 1980 CIA document *Soviet Covert Action and Propaganda*, a KGB manual is cited to indicate the nature and scope of Soviet strategic disinformation objectives:

> Strategic disinformation is directed at misleading the enemy concerning the basic questions of the state policy, the military-economic status, and the scientific-technical achievement of the Soviet Union; the policy of certain imperialist states with respect to each other and to other countries; and the specific counterintelligence tasks of the organs of state security.

I've given arguments here on why the Soviets would want to deceive us on the nature and deployment of their strategic nuclear weapons. As I've attempted to show, the impact of such deception on our current nuclear strategy may have been enormous: We may have been deprived of the most critical targeting information affecting our security; namely, Soviet offensive nuclear weapons whose undegraded employment can crucially degrade our ability to fight a nuclear war with Russia, to say nothing of increased U.S. civilian casualties resulting from Russia's undegraded Russian employment of nuclear weapons against us.

What about the rest of the PD-59 target list, dealing with control and power projection forces?

Soviet leadership, political and military, is a particularly important PD-59 target category, and therefore one where the Soviets can be expected to employ tactics of secrecy, cover, deception, and mobility to negate our preattack targeting. As our Defense Department recently observed: "Protection of their leadership has been a primary objective of the Soviets. . . . This protection has been achieved through the construction of deep, hard urban shelters and countless relocation sites." But how many of those relocation shelters are known and which would be occupied by the Soviet leadership in the event of nuclear war? In this connection, it is entirely conceivable that a complex of unknown shelters now exists that has completely escaped detection by our NTM.

A recent CIA study stated that identified fixed shelters of the Soviets were vulnerable to nuclear attack, which is hardly surprising in view of our present nuclear missile capabilities. If so, certainly having noted this claim, why would the Soviet leaders desire

49

to arrange for their execution by occupying these shelters in wartime, especially if they thought they were targeted? This wouldn't make any sense. So maybe they have been constructing decoy shelters to draw our attention, knowing we will see them being constructed, as a subterfuge to encourage the wasteful expenditure of our warheads, their real plans being to occupy only shelters believed to be unknown to U.S. nuclear planners. The importance of constructing decoy targets to draw both attention and fire is stressed in the Soviet literature, but rarely appears to be considered in our nuclear targeting analyses. We've always had a propensity for wanting to have hard evidence and have managed to convince ourselves that we have it, even when we don't.

Not only would such construction make good deception sense, it also would make good economic sense, in the event the unknown shelters became known. The cost to the United States to dispatch an ICBM warhead (say, an MX) to destroy a hardened target has escalated to tens of millions of dollars per warhead: vastly more expensive than the cost of a hardened shelter. This suggests the possibility of a large proliferation of shelters for Soviet leaders and raises additional questions about the ability of U.S. nuclear targeters to implement the PD-59 strategy against one of its most important target categories.

The Soviets have placed great emphasis on the need to disperse and duplicate critical facilities and move them on the eve of the war. In this connection, mobility becomes especially important, and when undertaken in anticipation of an enemy nuclear strike even has a special name, antiatomic maneuvers. Such ploys are intended to negate the effectiveness of the enemy's strike simply by moving targeted items, such as military units, weapons and ammunition stockpiles (especially nuclear munitions), air and missile defenses, control centers, communication facilities, transportation assets, and so forth; all of which could enhance their ability to project power in and out of the Soviet Union.

Recently, a key Pentagon official in the office of the secretary of defense explained the consequences of Soviet mobility: "Our ability to retaliate effectively against Soviet military assets is also no longer as clear as it once was. Their conventional military forces and nuclear reserves are protected by mobility. Although we could retaliate against the peacetime locations of such military units, there is doubt that such action would eliminate the fighting capability of the Soviet forces."

The Soviets hold it to be crucial that in the event of a nuclear war, their military forces necessary for both internal and external control be able to survive enemy nuclear strikes and be able to project their power during and after the war. Which is why the attack of these forces is high on the PD-59 target list. However, if our warheads are to impact on vacated bases and facilities, additional questions can be raised about the credibility of our military targeting strategy.

Several years ago, Sovietologist Richard Pipes, who had chaired the CIA's famous B Team on Soviet strategic objectives and later served on the National Security Council as resident Sovietologist, wrote on how the Soviets view nuclear war:

> Soviet nuclear strategy is counter*force* oriented. It targets for destruction—at any rate, in the initial strike—not the enemy's cities but his military forces and their command and communications facilities. Its primary aim is to destroy not civilians but soldiers and their leaders, and to undermine not so much the will to resist as the capability to do so.*

Pipes went on to say:

> Soviet theorists regard strategic nuclear forces (organized since 1966 into a separate arm, the Strategic Rocket Forces) to be the decisive branch of the armed services, in the sense that the ultimate outcome of modern war would be settled by nuclear exchanges. But since nuclear war, in their view, must lead not only to the enemy's defeat but also to his destruction (i.e., his incapacity to offer further resistance), they consider it necessary to make preparations for the follow-up phase, which may entail a prolonged war of attrition. . . . The notion of an extended nuclear war is deeply embedded in Soviet thinking, despite its being dismissed by Western strategists who think of war as a one-two exchange.

And Pipes stressed the emphasis placed by the Soviets on *defense* against nuclear attack, in contrast to the antidefense attitude that has long prevailed in the United States:

> . . . the U.S. theory of mutual deterrence postulates that no effective defense can be devised against an all-out nuclear attack: it is this postulate that makes such a war appear totally irrational. In order

---

* Richard Pipes, "Why the Soviet Union Thinks It Could Fight and Win a Nuclear War," *Commentary,* July 1979.

to make this premise valid, American civilian strategists have argued against a civil-defense program, against the ABM, and against air defenses.

Nothing illustrates better the fundamental differences between the two strategic doctrines than their attitudes to defense against a nuclear attack. The Russians agreed to certain imprecisely defined limitations on ABM after they had initiated a program in this direction, apparently because they were unable to solve the technical problems involved and feared the United States would forge ahead in this field. However, they then proceeded to build a tight ring of anti-aircraft defenses around the country while also developing a serious program of civil defense.

. . . the Soviet Union does not regard civil defense to be exclusively for the protection of ordinary civilians. Its chief function seems to be to protect what in Russia are known as the "cadres," that is, the political and military leaders as well as industrial managers and skilled workers—those who could reestablish the political and economic system once the war was over. Judging by Soviet definitions, civil defense has as much to do with the proper functioning of the country during and immediately after the war as with holding down casualties. Its organization . . . seems to be a kind of shadow government charged with responsibility for administering the country under the extreme stresses of nuclear war and its immediate aftermath.

The point to be made, in summarizing Pipes' remarks, is that the Soviets seem to be far more serious about a PD-59-type strategy than we are ourselves. Not only do they have basically a counter-force strategy in mind, but they are doing everything required to make such a strategy work, especially in the direction of reducing the damage to their country from U.S. nuclear strikes—through active and passive defense—and keeping the country functioning, as a viable political and economic system, during and after the war. In other words, they plan to fight a nuclear war in the classical sense: to win and survive. In the face of all this, should a war take place that we can't fight, what could we do?

To begin with, if Soviet deception and disinformation practices had been as successful as has been conjectured here, we could do very little, if anything, to achieve our immediate military objectives, if for no other reason than that we simply would not have a credible military target system to attack. Soviet strategic nuclear weapons would be essentially immune to attack at the beginning of the war. As for targets that might possibly come into view of U.S. reconnaissance systems, as the war progresses, it can be expected that the Soviets will take all measures to preclude this possibility by attacking our satellites (which are extremely vulnerable) and employing their air defenses (the most massive in history) against our reconnaissance aircraft. We would effectively be fighting blindfolded—unless we were to revert to an assured destruction policy, which could ensure our extermination but not necessarily the Soviets'.

Even were the Soviets obligingly to refrain from depriving us of a target system and sportingly to present us with a panoply of targets at the beginning of and during a war, there is a fundamental flaw in the U.S. strategy, alluded to by Pipes, that would prevent us from implementing the PD-59 strategy. Lacking active defenses to reduce the extent of Soviet nuclear strikes and civil defense to protect the citizenry from the effects of those strikes, the American people, who have developed practically a pathological horror of nuclear war, would in all probability undergo a total societal collapse. It is hard to imagine their being willing to tolerate even a day of nuclear explosions and radioactive fallout, having no means of protecting themselves, let alone the weeks and months envisioned by PD-59 strategy. In such a horrendous situation, it is equally hard to imagine a U.S. president—if he is still alive; Soviet strategy places high priority on the quick destruction of U.S. political leadership in a nuclear war—being determined to carry on the war to a "satisfactory" conclusion.

For these kinds of reasons, it is difficult to see the United States, in its present overall posture for fighting a nuclear war with Russia, being able to fight such a war. As things now stand, we may have little choice but to rest our hopes on deterrence and reshape our nuclear posture in a manner which best enhances this objective. And just in case deterrence fails some day, if we can't realistically prepare to fight a nuclear war, we should at least take proper measures to be able to cope with the Soviet war-fighting capabilities and, most important, *survive*. However, at least as important as reshaping our nuclear posture is the compelling necessity to eliminate our policy of containing the Red Army overseas so that we stand the most realistic way of avoiding nuclear war.

In the nuclear age, the old military maxim "The best defense is a good offense" has, in effect, dictated U.S. nuclear strategy and military requirements. Were we forced into a nuclear war as of today, the great bulk of our military effort would be directed toward offensive operations along the lines of PD-59; that is, unless the Soviets were to attack U.S. cities, which is not in their strategy. However, if we will be unable to conduct such operations, because we lack a credible target system, it becomes imperative for us drastically to change our strategy according to a new maxim, namely: "The best defense is a good defense." For the only time we may be able to see Soviet missiles and bombers and target them for attack will be when they are heading toward us. In fact, it may be that the only *moral* nuclear policy for the United States is one based primarily on *defense*, if the only target system we can establish in Russia consists of urban-industrial areas and other fixed installations directly related to the viability of the civilian population.

On March 24, 1983, Ronald Reagan, speaking to the American people, announced his decision to embark on a program of intensified research and development on antiballistic missile (ABM) weapons. "Would it not be better to save lives than to avenge them? Are we not capable of demonstrating our peaceful intentions by applying all our abilities and our ingenuity to achieving a truly lasting stability? I think we are—indeed, we must!" the president stated.

Many years earlier (in 1969), another American president, Richard Nixon, had made a similar, but far more forceful and concrete, policy statement on the need for ABM: "No president with the responsibility for the lives and security of the American people could fail to provide this protection." Nixon then proceeded to honor his responsibility to the American people by ordering the production of the Safeguard ABM system, which the Pentagon deemed to be highly effective. Three years later, however, he proceeded to abdicate his responsibility by signing the SALT I ABM treaty with the Soviets. The Safeguard program was stopped and with the great disincentive to moving forward on ABM the treaty provided, research and development on antimissile weapons were reduced to a snail's pace.

In the late 1960s the Soviets held to the high moral views of Reagan and Nixon on ABM. In 1967 Premier Aleksei Kosygin remarked: "I think that a defensive system, which prevents attack, is not a cause of the arms race but represents a factor preventing the death of people. . . . An antimissile system may cost more than an offensive one, but it is intended not for killing people but for saving human lives." Although the Soviets ratified the ABM treaty, their research and development continued at a high level—far higher than ours. Many U.S. military analysts decided that they had entered into the treaty for the purpose of heading off the U.S. Safeguard program while preparing for a day when their own developments would allow an effective ABM deployment, which many analysts believe presently is being masqueraded as a nationwide mobile antiaircraft system (not covered by any arms-control agreement).

In the context of the discussion here on Soviet deception practices and their implications for U.S. nuclear policy, would not President Reagan's question, "Would it not be better to save lives than to avenge them?" become of critical importance. To this point, the fundamental case for defense becomes exactly this simple: why not try to defend the American people in the event of a nuclear attack?

If viewed in this basic human context, even a halfway effective ABM system (Defense Secretary Caspar Weinberger has claimed that current U.S. ABM technology can provide a system that destroys 50 percent of incoming missiles) might save many millions of American lives and trillions of dollars of their property. If this were possible, as Aleksei Kosygin viewed it, even were an ABM system to cost much more than offensive nuclear weapons, would not the lives and property that might be saved more, far more, than justify the high cost? Surely, the American Roman Catholic bishops, who have morally condemned the use of offensive strategic nuclear weapons because of the enormous toll in human lives they would take, would agree with this position.

Regarding U.S. air defenses, it is ironic that all the very considerable gains we have made have been applied to the defense (against Soviet aggression) of friends and allies abroad—in Europe, South Korea, the Persian Gulf, the Middle East, etc.—our own continental defenses, by official design and decision, long ago having been emasculated. It is more than ironic that these defensive capabilities have been directed to theaters overseas where, should conflict occur, we stand the best chance of being drawn into a nuclear war with Russia that we can't fight.

From time to time U.S. administrations have attempted to establish a national civil defense program. These attempts always have been defeated, the reason being that the media and U.S. nuclear-war politics always have viewed civil defense as basically unworkable and unable to protect the American people at any meaningful level. The facts of the matter, however, are that were the United States to move realistically on civil defense, an extremely effective system could be built: costing far less than active defense systems and capable of saving the lives of most Americans.

As the old saying goes: "What you don't know can't hurt you." In an age of intercontinental missiles and thermonuclear warheads the saying could be reworded: "What you don't know can kill you." Unless we change our nuclear policy and shift our nuclear emphasis to defending our country, what we don't know about the Soviet strategic nuclear capabilities may indeed bring about our national demise. And there is no way that pursuing treaties on nuclear arms control the way we have been pursuing them will reduce this risk.

4

Can Nuclear Arms Control Reduce the Risk of Nuclear War?

ONLY TWICE IN THE sorry history of our nuclear arms-control efforts have we realistically approached this matter. We were realistic because we were able to show some rare common sense about the Soviets and their penchant for secrecy. On each of these occasions we proposed that they open up their country to whatever degree of *inspection*, in contrast to *observation*, we deemed necessary. Needless to say, our proposals were rejected out of hand, for one simple reason: the Soviets were not about to let us know what they were up to in nuclear weaponry. And they're still not.

Right after World War II President Truman directed an advisory committee of distinguished Americans (including Robert Oppenheimer, who had directed the atomic bomb development at Los Alamos) to study the problem of international control of atomic energy, including nuclear weapons. The committee was under the leadership of Dean Acheson (then undersecretary of state and soon to become secretary) and David Lilienthal (who had become famous for helping establish public power and was soon to become the first chairman of the U.S. Atomic Energy Commission). From the committee's efforts came the first U.S. proposal for controlling the atom. This was in the form of the celebrated Baruch Plan, which sought to reach this objective through the creation of an international-control organization. The Baruch Plan, had it been implemented, would have achieved complete control of all aspects of atomic energy, from uranium ore deposits to final products—including atomic bombs. Its primary goal was to rid the world of nuclear weapons.

The Baruch Plan, which was adopted by the U.N. General Assembly in December 1946, couldn't have been tougher-minded regarding its enforcement provisions. All parties to the proposed agreement were to be subject to the most intrusive scrutiny by the international-control authority. The authority was to have the right to conduct aerial surveys of areas (to include military reservations) where uranium ore might be mined and processed, and ground explorations and inspections of these areas could be made to ensure compliance. "Freedom of access" by representatives of the authority was held essential to the success of this plan.

In his statement to the United Nations, Bernard Baruch could hardly understate the necessity to ensure adherence to the proposed agreement:

> We must provide the mechanism to assure that atomic energy is used for peaceful purposes and preclude its use in war. To that end, we must provide immediate, swift, and sure punishment of those who violate the agreements that are reached by the nations. Penalization is essential if peace is to be more than a feverish interlude between wars. And, too, the United Nations can prescribe individual responsibility and punishment on the principles applied at Nuremberg . . . a formula certain to benefit the world's future.

To put it mildly, the United States was being grimly serious about nuclear arms control in 1946—a far cry from our current position where verification procedures are determined by what the Soviets are willing to grant us, treaty violations by the Soviets are effectively ignored, and punishment (heaven forbid!) is no longer discussed in diplomatic circles. In fact, Bernard Baruch felt so strongly about enforcement of his plan that he more than hinted at the need to punish violators even by "nuking" them in some cases, regardless of how the U.N. Security Council might have felt.

Needless to say, the U.S. proposal was rejected by the Soviets (who already had begun, with a vehemence, the development of their own nuclear weapons, culminating in their first nuclear explosion a scant three years after). Whatever the underlying reasons for the Soviet decision may have been, they have remained conjectural and contentious. However, implicit in the decision was a rejection of full inspection of their territory.

A decade later, the United States, while resigned to the continuing development and production of nuclear weapons, again sought to control them—this time it hoped to prevent their use through surprise attack. On this occasion, though, the United States, having made great strides in aerial photographic reconnaissance (for example, the U-2 high-altitude spyplane), was willing to conclude an agreement that did not call for inspectors—"legal spies"—on the ground. Inspectors in airplanes would suffice. And from this belief came President Dwight Eisenhower's bold "open-skies" proposal in 1955, seeking to prevent nuclear surprise attack as a serious military option.

Addressing the Geneva Conference of Heads of Government on July 21, 1955, Eisenhower said:

> No sound and reliable agreement can be made unless it is completely covered by an inspection and reporting system adequate to support every portion of the agreement. The lessons of history teach us that disarmament agreements without adequate reciprocal inspection increase the dangers of war and do not brighten the prospects of peace. . . . I propose, therefore, that we take a practical step, that we begin an arrangement, very quickly, as between ourselves—immediately. The steps would include: To give to each other a complete blueprint of our military establishments, from beginning to end, from one end of our countries to the other; lay out the establishments and provide the blueprints to each other. Next, to provide within our countries facilities for aerial photography to the other country—we to provide you the facilities within our country, ample facilities for aerial reconnaissance, where you can make all the pictures you choose and take them to your own country to study, you to provide exactly the same facilities for us and we to make these examinations, and by this step to convince the world that we are providing as between ourselves against the possibility of great surprise attack, thus lessening danger and relaxing tension. Likewise we will make more easily attainable a comprehensive and effective system of inspection and disarmament, because what I propose, I assure you, would be but a beginning.

The Soviets rejected the Eisenhower proposal ostensibly on the grounds that it represented arms control without disarmament; the U.S. plan did not contain a promise for actual reductions in nuclear weapons. However, once again there seemed to be a continuation of the ingrained Soviet attitude toward secrecy and concealment of everything of military significance going on in the USSR; namely, a rejection of effective inspection by the potential adversary. In this case, such inspection would have been accomplished through a "violation" of Soviet airspace, which was not acceptable to the Soviets: witness the shooting down of the U-2 a few years later and the furor that resulted.

Were the Soviets genuinely to have had a concern over the possibility of nuclear surprise attack—they claimed they did and were forever charging that the United States was planning such an attack against them—they should have jumped at the Eisenhower proposal. Surely, a fear of nuclear holocaust should have transcended whatever fears they might have had that prying U.S. "eyes in the sky" might ferret out some of their military secrets. But their alleged obsession with nuclear secrecy seemed to prevail over nuclear sanity. Or was it actually the contrary situation—namely, that they sought a surprise attack capability for themselves, which could be achieved only through secrecy? One should keep in mind that no tenet of Soviet military doctrine has been expressed more often and more strongly than *surprise*.

With the Soviet renunciation of the open-skies proposal, the United States should have been darkly suspicious that the Soviets viewed nuclear arms control mainly in the context of military advantage to them. They may not have shared the U.S. philosophy that arms-control treaties are of advantage to both sides in supposedly reducing the risk of war. However, the prevailing U.S. attitude was that arms control was a logical imperative that transcended narrow selfish national objectives and that the Soviets had grasped this logic. So we continued with this noble quest—and still do.

Two months before the U.S. open-skies proposal, the Soviets for the first time had stated a desire for a comprehensive nuclear test ban treaty (CTBT), which, in principle, would have foreclosed on *all* nuclear testing. In a May 11, 1955, statement to the United Nations the Soviets proposed that "states possessing atomic and hydrogen weapons shall undertake to discontinue tests of these weapons." But they showed no signs of being willing to open up their country to inspection of suspected areas of violation, and still don't. Yet, three years later the United States entered into CTBT negotiations with the Soviet Union; more than a quarter century later the negotiations remain unresolved, because the verification issues remain unresolved. Regarding this continuing impasse, a fair question might be asked: Have the Soviets been concerned more with being caught in a test violation than with our finding out what they have been testing, or vice versa? This point is brought up here and will be brought up again, because it penetrates to the heart of the nuclear arms-control matter. If arms control is to have any real meaning for our national security interests, what really counts is knowing what the other side is doing, not whether a treaty is being violated. If we don't know what the other side is doing, how can we reassure ourselves that a given treaty is working toward a stable nuclear balance, which is supposed to be our primary arms-control objective?

By 1963, when the frustrations over the CTBT negotiations had produced a deep political schism in the United States—because of the verification issue—David Lilienthal, who had been an impassioned arms-control advocate for many years, became highly skeptical over the nuclear disarmament process. In this mood he delivered a speech (in March of that year) at Princeton University entitled "The Mythology of Nuclear Disarmament." A key part of his speech follows:

> I believe it to be fundamental that it is the cause of war that must first be ameliorated before we can safely make progress toward eliminating or even limiting substantially those terrible weapons of war. The reason nuclear weapons are a threat to the world lies not in the inanimate weapons themselves, but in the animosities, the suspicions, the conflicting drives and ambitions and ideologies of the nations who possess the weapons. . . .
>
> The fantastic destructive power of the atom is a reality. The conclusions drawn from this fact are myths. Those myths are still at the foundation of our policies and our outlook.

On the U.S. side, although partly refuted by a record showing that we indeed possess these undue qualities listed by Lilienthal (animosity, suspicion, etc.), Americans tend to view their country as extremely trustworthy in observing disarmament treaties. After all, we are an open society; the government puts out an enormous amount of information on our nuclear-weapon capabilities; and any devious behavior by us to avert the terms of agreement almost certainly would be leaked to the media by someone within the government. The United States is, to a first approximation, an open book.

On the Soviet side, there is an overwhelming amount of evidence showing longstanding propensities for secrecy and disinformation, and a record of breaking or violating treaties. These propensities should have cast into serious doubt the U.S. assessment on Soviet objectives for their nuclear-weapon developments and entering into and observing nuclear arms control agreements. But this was not to be the case (and still isn't), for shortly after Lilienthal's admonitions came out, we signed the first nuclear arms-control treaty with the Soviets, the Limited Test Ban Treaty (August 1963). The treaty banned nuclear tests in the atmosphere, in outer space, and under water; it thereby consigned all testing underground.

From our point of view, the treaty represented a great success. We told ourselves that we finally had broken ice and now could look forward to a series of agreements for constraining and reducing nuclear stockpiles. From the Russian point of view, the treaty also was heralded as a great success for the nuclear disarmament process. However, the Soviets may have had another reason for being so enthusiastic; namely, the U.S. had put itself into a position where it no longer could determine what the Russians might be up to in their nuclear-warhead developments. Within reason we could tell whether they were violating the treaty; but at the same time we had foreclosed on our ability to monitor their warhead programs.

Before the treaty was signed, the Russians, like ourselves, had conducted the great bulk of their tests in the atmosphere. This gave us the chance to collect debris from these tests, analyze it, and get an idea of what had been tested. Now, however, by the terms of the treaty, there was to be no debris escaping into the air. Thus there was nothing to collect and analyze. As a Pentagon official (who advised the secretary of defense on nuclear-weapon matters) explained the situation several years after the treaty was signed:

> We have little certain knowledge of the Soviet warhead designs, of their vulnerability, or of Soviet testing or development philosophy. . . . We do not know what the Soviets have accomplished in their test program since 1963, but unless their program was a very sterile one, the Soviets would almost certainly be in a far more favorable position to upgrade their future stockpile with even more effective tactical and strategic systems.

Although we may have signed an enforceable treaty, in so doing we made it impossible to figure out whether the Russians were falling behind us, catching up with us, or outdistancing us in warhead technology. How, therefore, could anybody argue that the treaty was in the direction of providing greater security for us when our ignorance in such a critical area was so great? How could anybody argue that we were moving responsibly toward the consummation of another nuclear arms agreement when we had deprived ourselves of such vital knowledge, unquestionably essential for devising a sound negotiating strategy?

For example, several years ago it was reported that a Soviet underground nuclear testing facility had been observed that looked suspiciously like a nuclear particle beam development directed toward an antimissile capability. But since we didn't have access to what was going on inside this facility, all we could do was conjecture. Could it be that indeed the Soviets (long before President Reagan gave his famous "Star Wars" speech last year, making a fervent plea for getting such a defensive capability) had begun such a program holding such fateful consequences for our security? We don't know and can't know, because we signed a nuclear arms-control treaty more than twenty years ago that ruled out our ability to know. And there may be more such examples of Soviet nuclear-weapon development that we can't check on, or even conjecture about.

The second nuclear accords came nine years later (1972) when the Nixon administration signed agreements with the Soviets affecting each side's strategic nuclear weapons arsenals. SALT I consisted of two basic parts: (1) an interim agreement providing limitations on strategic offensive nuclear armaments; and (2) a treaty sharply limiting the development and deployment of anti-ballistic missile (ABM) systems.

The offensive arms limitation agreement basically placed ceilings on the numbers of strategic ballistic missile *launchers;* not missiles, which most people thought was the case, and which the administration, somewhat guilefully, let them think was the case.

In effect, it froze the number of ICBM silos and the number of submarines capable of launching nuclear ballistic missiles. Of these two missile categories, by far and away the ICBMs were held to be the more important, representing a much greater military capability than the submarine-launched missiles (SLBMs). As a consequence, in signing this agreement, the U.S. once again had fallen (or had been deceptively pushed by the Soviets) into the trap of accepting an agreement that deprived it of critical knowledge about Soviet nuclear capabilities. For the only concrete knowledge (if

63

you'll excuse the pun) we had of their ICBM deployments was the existence of some fourteen hundred concrete-lined holes in the ground, whose construction the Soviets so obligingly had let us see with our spy satellites. As explained in the previous chapter, there is no way that we can determine whether the silos contain missiles, and there are compelling military reasons for the Soviets not to have filled their silos with missiles.

Moreover, if the Soviets had actually deployed their ICBMs elsewhere, in no way would this have been a violation of the limitations agreement they signed with us. The only thing they agreed to limit was the number of holes in the ground; there was no stipulation whatsoever on limiting missiles. We had convinced ourselves that silos and missiles had a one-to-one correlation and the Soviets, who must have been both delighted and amazed by our naiveté, did nothing to dissuade us from this conviction. If we were crazy enough, because of our obsession over consummating arms-control agreements, to sign such an agreement, the Russians certainly weren't crazy enough to tell us how crazy we were.

What I'm getting at here is that in signing the offensive arms-limitation agreement in SALT I, we simply did not know what we were up to. For public consumption and to ensure congressional approval (which was overwhelming), the administration put forth this agreement as a verifiable numbers game. The truth of the matter, however, was that we didn't know how to count, and still don't. We sought to convince ourselves that the agreement yielded nuclear parity in strategic weapon capabilities, and thus provided a nuclear equilibrium between ourselves and the Russians. In truth, however, we had given the Russians a license to achieve nuclear superiority without even running the risk of violating the agreement.

If we caught them at what we would regard as skullduggery but what they would regard as their right to do what they were allowed to do, what could we do?

Well, we could go through the same recriminations against them as we did back in 1961. This was when they broke what we thought was a gentlemen's agreement not to test nuclear weapons, and resumed such testing on the most massive scale in history. So we lambasted the living daylights out of them, and then, a few months later, resumed test ban talks with them.

Or we could threaten to increase our buildup of ICBMs, to match theirs. However, we would probably do no more than threaten, since it would make no military sense to build up just for the sake of building up: lacking a target system to justify the buildup. What we really ought to do, upon seeing signs of such deception by the Soviets, is direct our spleen at ourselves for having been such damned fools.

In the offensive arms-limitation agreement was a unilateral U.S. statement that we "would consider the deployment of operational land-mobile ICBM launchers . . . as inconsistent with the objectives of that agreement." It just so happens that around this time the Soviets had embarked upon their SS-20 program and a few years later we began (or thought we began) to observe this missile being deployed. As has been discussed here, there are a number of sound military reasons for believing that the SS-20 always has been a mobile ICBM; and at the time of SALT I we possessed more than sufficient evidence of the Soviet theater nuclear-weapons programs for us to understand these reasons. Nevertheless, in our self-inflicted ignorance we registered our official objections to the Soviets' deploying mobile ICBMs and blithely assumed that they would accede; which in all probability they haven't.

We chose to believe, and the Soviets chose to let us believe, that the SS-20 was an intermediate-range ballistic missile (IRBM) directed primarily against targets in Europe and Asia. The probable truth of the matter, however, was that it was a mobile ICBM directed primarily against us. As of today, it is entirely possible that thousands of SS-20 warheads are deployed around the USSR capable of hitting thousands of targets in the United States. So here's still another example of how we manage to get into nuclear arms-control agreements where we don't know what we're getting into; and once we do get into them, we are unable to find out what we've done.

In 1972, after a long and mainly irrational attack by those factions in the U.S. scientific community and the media who almost blindly favored nuclear arms control for its own sake, President Richard Nixon backed away from his commitment to provide an ABM defense for the American people. Instead, he accepted Russian proposals to prohibit a nationwide ABM capability and then proceeded to formalize this acceptance by signing the ABM treaty in Moscow. By his own previous avowals to protect American lives, in signing this treaty Nixon was guilty of a moral travesty. By practically any other civilized standards, he was equally guilty; for on what conceivable grounds could a concrete effort guaranteed to save human lives be discarded in favor of a disarmament treaty that guaranteed the loss of human lives in case of war? Especially when the record of such treaties through recorded history has been so appalling and filled with deceit by hostile nations, like the Soviet Union, which have exploited them to gain military advantage and often have gone to war with those peaceable nations, like ourselves, which have been so gullible as to enter into them. And in signing the ABM treaty, the U.S. not only abandoned a moral position it had held throughout its history, but did so in dangerous disregard of Soviet motivations and deceptive practices.

Before the ABM treaty, the Soviets had emphatically extolled the virtues of national self-defense and ABM systems. The military doctrine of the USSR had held the defense of the state to be an indispensable component of state security. In accordance with this doctrinal requirement, the Soviets had constructed an extensive air-defense network (the most extensive in history) around the USSR and were building up a nationwide civil defense system. All told, the various defensive measures the Soviets were taking at that time may have consumed about half the total strategic force budget. (I might point out here that civil defense in the USSR is regarded as a critical component of Soviet strategic capabilities. It is under the jurisdiction of the Soviet military and is organized and run by a very large military command.)

This being the case, on what conceivable grounds would the Soviets have wanted to deprive themselves of a ballistic missile defense system, leaving themselves vulnerable to devastation by our missiles, when they already had applied themselves so massively to defense against bomber attacks? It just didn't seem consistent with their long held doctrine and practice. Why, at the same time, didn't they propose a treaty barring air defense as well (which we would have been delighted to sign), if the spirit of SALT I meant doing away with defense against nuclear attack?

Or was it more likely that the Soviets had no intention of foresaking defense against missile attack and were masquerading their forbidden ABM program under their permissible air-defense program? (As most likely they were doing in masquerading their forbidden SS-20 ICBM program as a permissible IRBM program for use in the Eurasian theater.) Having had such a firm requirement for ABM defenses, the logic behind such deception would have been almost overwhelming to the Soviets.

To be sure, in negotiating the ABM treaty those so engaged in Washington considered the possibility that the Soviets might improve their air-defense missiles to a degree where they held a respectable ABM capability. However, the pressures, coming from the top, to achieve a treaty were so great that concerns over this possibility were effectively dismissed.

For example, the prevailing protreaty faction made claims that the Soviets lacked sufficient production of fissile material —specifically, plutonium—to enable producing the required number of nuclear warheads for a significant ABM system. However, the facts were that we didn't know enough about Soviet plutonium production facilities to verify such claims. Nor, for that matter—for reasons brought out previously—did we know enough about Soviet nuclear-warhead technology to be able to determine how much plutonium might go into an ABM warhead. (If we don't know how much plutonium goes into a Soviet ABM warhead, how can we know how many warheads they might build?) So we had on our hands an intelligence mess in which ignorance was being compounded by more ignorance: hardly a responsible way to arrive at so crucial a decision; but that's the way the game was being played—politically.

As to whether the Soviets might have been seriously restrained in plutonium production when the ABM treaty was being negotiated, what evidence we have suggests the contrary. Most signs point to the probability that Soviet nuclear power reactors were designed primarily to produce plutonium for nuclear warheads, power production being a secondary consideration. In which case, the Soviets today could have far greater amounts of plutonium for ABM warheads than the United States has been willing to grant them. Had U.S. officials been responsibly concerned over this possibility when negotiating the ABM treaty, they could have reminded themselves of what Vice President Richard Nixon was told in 1959 while visiting a Soviet nuclear reactor facility. At that time, the chief engineer of the facility told Nixon: "We of the Soviet Union do not believe nuclear power is the most important way of obtaining electrical energy." There couldn't have been a stronger clue than this to the Soviets' real intentions for their supposedly peaceful nuclear reactor program; namely, that it was basically a program for producing swords, not plowshares.

Even though the possibility of the Soviets' pursuing an ABM project via improved air-defense missiles was effectively dismissed by the prevailing forces in Washington, that possibility was nevertheless included in the ABM treaty language, in article 6:

To enhance assurance of the effectiveness of the limitations on ABM

67

systems and their components provided by the Treaty, each Party undertakes:

(a) not to give missiles, launches, or radars, other than ABM interceptor missiles, ABM launchers, or ABM radars, capabilities to counter strategic ballistic missiles or their elements in flight trajectory, and not to test them in an ABM mode; and

(b) not to deploy in the future radars for early warning of strategic ballistic missile attack except at locations along the periphery of its national territory and oriented outward.

Put in less technical terms, article 6 said in effect that the Soviets were not permitted to improve their air-defense missiles and test them against incoming ballistic missile warheads; and they were not to deploy radars that could track incoming warheads and direct defensive missiles against them. Having agreed not to do this, the Soviets proceeded to do it; to what extent we don't know, but we know enough to believe that they did and still do.

At what juncture we may have seen enough to convince ourselves that an actual nationwide ABM deployment exists in the USSR, who knows? Because of Soviet deceptive practices, we may never be able to see enough. But because of our unrealistic attitude in approaching the ABM issue, such a deployment may be a very distinct and dangerous possibility. In fact, when one considers the present attitude of the Soviets toward nuclear arms control, as a result of the U.S. Euromissile deployment, there is a distinct probability that they may use the deployment as an excuse to withdraw from the ABM treaty.

In the SALT II treaty, signed in 1979, limitations were placed on the total number of both ballistic missiles and heavy bombers capable of conducting strategic strikes on the U.S. and the USSR. On the Soviet side, the bombers covered by the treaty were two aircraft of ancient vintage; the Bear and Bison bombers had been in the force for almost a quarter century. The Backfire bomber, which we have discussed, was excluded on the basis of a Soviet pledge that it was designed to be operated strictly as a medium bomber incapable of missions against the United States. President Leonid Brezhnev, to show his sincerity, went so far as to hand to President Jimmy Carter a written statement that avowed:

The Soviet side informs the US side that the Soviet "Tu-22M" airplane, called "Backfire" in the USA, is a medium-range bomber, and that it does not intend to give this airplane the capability of operating

68

at intercontinental distances. In this connection, the Soviet side states that it will not increase the radius of action of this airplane in such a way as to enable it to strike targets on the territory of the USA. Nor does it intend to give it such a capability in any other manner, including by in-flight refueling. At the same time, the Soviet side states that it will not increase the production rate of this airplane as compared to the present rate.

Further to allay U.S. fears that Backfire might ultimately constitute a substantial strategic bomber force, Brezhnev promised that its production rate would not exceed thirty per year. President Carter publicly stated that the U.S. considered the carrying out of this commitment by Brezhnev essential to the obligations assumed under SALT II.

In the six years since SALT II was signed, disturbing signs have cropped up, indicating that the Soviets had deceived us on their stated intentions for Backfire. It recently has been revealed that two squadrons of these bombers were being deployed in Arctic staging bases, where, even with the range we agreed to accept, extensive coverage over U.S. targets could be achieved. In addition, it has been reported that Backfire production may be as much as one third greater than the level Brezhnev promised not to exceed. Since it is very difficult to conceal bombers that, in contrast to missiles, do have to fly during peacetime, it is not too surprising that we detected these infractions. However, what should be of real concern to us is that this deceit by the Soviets may be only a part of a massive pattern in which a number of nuclear-weapon systems (discussed previously) have been misrepresented to us and successfully concealed to date.

As has been pointed out, just as for the SS-20, for the Soviets to add Backfire to their already huge and modernized force of theater nuclear weapons would seem to have no logical underpinnings. Furthermore, short of having a Soviet Backfire ever defect to the West, where we could determine for ourselves what the actual performance of this airplane is, there has been no way for us to check on the veracity of Brezhnev's statement. As in so many other cases, we accepted the Soviets' word on the basis of ignorance and our unabated zeal to gain agreements. We seem never to learn.

Putting aside for the moment our proclivity to negotiate agreements without real knowledge of what the Soviets may have been up to in their nuclear weapon developments, let us view another cause for alarm: In seeking arms-control solutions to nuclear-war issues, we have never squarely faced up to the issue of nuclear war, nor have we accepted the fact that the Soviets always have faced up to this issue. Instead, allegedly in our security interests, we have sought either to preclude certain developments such as nuclear testing, or ABM deployments, or mobile ICBMs—all of which, realistically pursued, would *enhance* our security interests—or to limit or reduce (such as missile and bomber deployments) developments whose limitation or reduction, improperly pursued, would greatly reduce our security interests, without any real idea of what we were trying to accomplish. It was assumed, practically as an article of faith, that moving forward—that is, negotiating agreements—in the arms-control process was moving in the direction of reducing the risk of nuclear war and thereby increasing our security.

Why this was so (especially in view of the wretched history of disarmament agreements, history in which practically all agreements, sooner or later, were followed by still another war) was never made clear. Rather, as David Lilienthal finally came to realize, controlling nuclear weapons was superstitiously equated with trying to destroy or curtail a threatening mythological monster. We simply refused to come to grips with the real world around us and the real threat to our security: the behavior of human beings (including ourselves) and nations (including our own).

If stopping nuclear testing, which has been an official U.S. policy for the past quarter century, deprives us, or our key allies, of obtaining highly discriminate warheads that pose no threat of the nuclear doomsday so widely heralded these days, why is this an ingrained virtue and a boon to our security? Or if stopping testing precluded possibilities for defensive nuclear warheads that could substantially reduce the damage to our country in the event of nuclear attack, how can this be construed as reducing the risk of war and improving our security?

Precluding the establishment of defenses against nuclear ballistic missiles, as we did with the 1972 ABM treaty (which was hailed as the most important arms-control treaty of the nuclear age), has not succeeded in reducing the risk of Soviet nuclear attack against us. In the thirteen years since the ABM treaty was signed, successive U.S. administrations have warned of the increased Soviet nuclear threat against our increasingly vulnerable nuclear retaliatory forces—hardly indicative of a reduced threat of nuclear war. And if the upshot of the ABM treaty was President Reagan's impassioned moral plea last year to save lives rather than avenge them by developing an ABM capability, then stopping ABM, via the 1972 treaty, would seem to have been more a moral dereliction than a virtue.

Precluding the deployment of mobile ICBMs in SALT I was hailed as a move toward increasing our security. The result was, as just discussed, that our fixed-based ICBMs proceeded to become dangerously vulnerable to a Soviet first strike, forcing the development of the MX missile, which was required to be invulnerable to a first strike. However, when it turned out that Congress would not accept the proposed invulnerable MX deployment modes of the Carter and Reagan administrations, all of a sudden a great passion for a mobile ICBM emerged. As a result, the mobile Midgetman ICBM development is now proceeding with full blessing by almost everyone in the Congress, including some of the most impassioned nuclear arms controllers. In retrospect, the SALT I provision to forbid mobile ICBMs was not only ill advised, but downright stupid, in light of how our security since has been affected.

In the limitation and reduction game, we have been playing a numbers game wherein counting numbers of weapons has become a substitute for trying to understand what game we should be playing with these weapons. Or, more important, what game the Soviets have been playing with us. Specifically, the Soviet game plan for nuclear arms control, from the very beginning, may have been little more than to exploit the process: to achieve a stretchout of U.S. nuclear-weapon developments in certain areas, to force cancellation of other developments (such as ABM and mobile ICBMs), and to effect limitations on still others; while all along carrying out, through secrecy and deception, an uninhibited across-the-board program of their own to achieve a decisive superiority enabling them to win and survive a nuclear war, should it ever occur.

From the time we laid down our silo-based Minuteman ICBM program (intended to be an invulnerable replacement for the highly vulnerable first-generation Atlas missile) until it became operational encompassed but a handful of years. And it was around the time that Minuteman became operational that we began our first serious major venture in nuclear arms control—in the early 1960s. Convinced that the Soviets could not possibly build up their nuclear strength to our level, because of their crippled economy and pressing domestic needs, ranking officials in the Kennedy administration argued that if we would stop our buildup and delay on new ICBM developments, we could bring the Soviets to the bargaining table and negotiate a nuclear arms-limitation treaty—in our favor, no less. We could eat our cake and have it: achieve arms control and keep our strategic nuclear superiority. To give you an idea of our official thinking around that time here is what our secretary of defense, Robert McNamara, said in 1965: "The Soviets have decided that they have lost the quantitative race and they are not seeking to engage us in that contest . . . there is no indication that the Soviets are seeking to develop a strategic nuclear force as large as our own."

The Russians, however, didn't care to snap at the bait implicit in McNamara's statement and sign up for arms control. Nor did they seem to believe what McNamara had told them about the futility of their efforts to catch up with us, for three years later Harold Brown, secretary of the air force, testified (unhappily) before the Congress, complaining:

> You see, we leveled out our missile force. We announced how big our missile force was going to be. Our plans are that five years from now we will have just about as many missiles as we have right now. They have known that. They have known it for a couple of years, and they keep on building.

By 1969 the Soviets apparently had amassed a sufficiently large nuclear capability, which consisted mainly of ICBMs, to give them a decent arms-control negotiating position. They privately expressed a willingness to enter into what became the SALT I talks. However, they also kept building up their nuclear forces, still emphasizing ICBMs, while we still kept ours at the same level. This situation continued until we signed the SALT I accords in 1972. By then the Minuteman missile had been in the force for over ten years.

Now believing that the Russians genuinely shared our arms-control convictions, although we set about studying requirements for replacing Minuteman with a more effective modernized ICBM, we elected to stay with Minuteman in the spirit of seeking another arms-control agreement representing significant advances over SALT I. But while the Russians were more than willing to continue the SALT process, they showed no willingness whatsoever to delay developing new ICBMs. They quickly moved ahead on a family of new missiles, which today constitute the bulk of their strategic nuclear strength—while we remained with Minuteman, which will not be replaced by a new survivable ICBM until the 1990s. If then.

72

A sad illustration it is of how we become paralyzed toward maintaining our security because of an unrealistic zeal over nuclear arms control.

Limiting nuclear weapons by themselves without limiting all the other factors that relate to the conduct and outcome of a nuclear war represents not only unsound arms control, but unsound defense planning. And if we don't know what is really being limited on the Soviet side, or whether anything is being limited at all, a limitations agreement based on such ignorance becomes downright foolhardy. Such agreement can seriously, even fatally, endanger our security. In the two SALT offensive arms-limitations agreements we have entered into and chosen to observe, even though we are not legally bound to do so, we have committed the folly of avoiding objective consideration of the nuclear-war issue. We have done this because we don't really believe that nuclear war is possible. We haven't truly cared how much, if at all, the agreements were limiting the Soviets' military capabilities, again because we haven't really believed nuclear war to be possible.

These limitations agreements were based on our supposed ability to count numbers of nuclear weapons, but our real underlying attitude always has been that numbers don't count. When the Congress has decided that an agreement was unacceptable because it gave the Russians a bigger weapon count than ourselves, the real reason was that the Russians had done something nasty, like invading Afghanistan after SALT II had been signed. However, when the Russian nastiness had been forgotten (even though still going on), we would revert to form and go along with the agreement. (Witness presidential candidate Ronald Reagan vehemently denouncing SALT II because the numbers were unfair to us; President Ronald Reagan saying that "linkage," with Soviet nastiness, would underlie his approach to nuclear arms control, and refusing to negotiate; and, a little later, when domestic political pressures for resuming negotiations began to threaten his political position, the president not only scrapping linkage but agreeing to observe the terms of SALT II; and still later, when the Russians committed one of their nastiest deeds by shooting down Korean Airline Flight 007, the president simultaneously expressing his horror and outrage and proclaiming that in no way would that atrocity affect continuing nuclear arms-control talks, which a few months later the Russians deserted.) All these shenanigans have been tolerated by the Congress and the American people because they too have never believed in the numbers game.

So what if the Russians had more and bigger missiles than we did, what difference did it make, if we still had enough to blow them up several times over? Which translated into our retaliatory ability to wipe practically every Soviet city and town off the map, kill more than a hundred million Russian people, and devastate their economy to boot, even though our government's policy rules out such a reprisal. Which in turn translated into the inviolability of our deterrent strategy: there won't be, there can't be, nuclear war, because it is too horrible to happen. The trouble is, however, the Soviets never have shared this view; they have accepted the dismal fact that, as in *The Day After*, human bellicosity and irrationality are still with us in the nuclear age, and that nuclear war is distinctly possible. They have been taking all the necessary measures, including manipulating our nuclear arsenal through arms-control negotiations, to ensure that they can survive *The Day After*. Perhaps they can. But if we continue to place our hopes for avoiding nuclear war so heavily on nuclear arms control as we have been practicing it, there will come a day when almost surely they can—and when certainly we can't.

Whereas there is not an iota's worth of evidence to show that a quarter century of nuclear arms-control negotiations and agreements have in any way resulted in reducing the threat of nuclear war (which most Americans, when polled nowadays, think is at an all-time high), one result has been that the horror of nuclear war has been reduced. At first glance, this would seem to benefit all parties concerned; but a little reflection shows that the Soviets may have been benefited far more than we, to our great disadvantage.

To what extent the horror for us has been reduced, since our ignorance of Soviet nuclear capabilities has been so great, we really don't know. On the other hand, the horror for the Russians, from our weapons, has been reduced very considerably, for two reasons: (1) the destructive potential of the U.S. arsenal has decreased appreciably; and (2) having continuously improved their offensive and defensive capabilities for fighting a nuclear war, and having placed limits, through arms-control agreements, on the size of the U.S. nuclear retaliatory capability, the Russians are now in a much better position to limit the devastation to their country.

For these reasons, contrary to President Reagan's repeated claims that both sides can only lose a nuclear war, a day will come (if it hasn't already come) when the Soviets will both win (in a military sense) and survive (in a socioeconomic sense) a nuclear war with us. As for winning, as has already been explained, in all probability the Soviets long have had this capability in the bag. As for surviving, if they continue to improve their first-strike capabilities against our ICBM and bomber forces; modernize their air defenses and deploy an ABM system; and, of critical importance, expand their civil defense (to include protecting their political leadership) and industrial recovery capabilities;* then their survival against a U.S. retaliatory ability that has been limited (in offensive weapons) and hamstrung (in defensive weapons) by arms-control agreements will be reasonably ensured.

If we remain bound and determined to pursue nuclear arms control, it will be grimly essential for our security and survival that we make two basic changes in our approach to the subject. First, we will have to revise our nuclear policies to take into account those of the Soviets. Second, we will have to return to the realities we briefly recognized right after World War II and demand that any nuclear arms-control agreement be preceded by full inspection of each side's nuclear capabilities, to ensure that the agreement has meaning and is in our security interests. Unless we take these two steps, to stake our hopes on arms control as the best way to reduce the risk of nuclear war will be the worst path we can take. In fact, even were we to scrap arms control (or the Russians did it for us, which they recently came close to doing), if we did not take the first step our future would be bleak indeed.**

If we are to continue negotiating nuclear arms-control treaties, what first has to be done, which we've never done in the treaties we've negotiated to date, is to figure out just what we should be negotiating. The answer, of course, is that we should be negotiating primarily to enhance our national security.

Our arms-control negotiators, of course, would vehemently deny

---

* The Pentagon has testified before the Congress that as of now the Soviet leadership possesses "enough bunkers and supporting communications . . . to have odds of surviving if targeted by our most numerous and survivable [warheads]"; and that their measures to protect their industrial capacity may succeed in reducing the destructive area of our warheads "by as much as 99 percent." There is considerable evidence pointing to the fact that in-place hardened urban shelters already can accommodate some forty-five million Soviet city dwellers, and that within the next ten years three-fourths of the urban population will be so protected.

** Winston Churchill once wrote: "However absorbed a commander may be in the elaboration of his own thoughts, it is necessary sometimes to take the enemy into consideration." Which precisely describes the absurdity of our comportment in nuclear arms control.

75

that they've been doing anything else. The truth of the matter is, though, they've been doing practically everything else, because they simply haven't known what they've been doing. Accordingly, they have been negotiating around a U.S. policy that assumed a make-believe world; an appraisal of Soviet nuclear policy that the Soviets have never held for themselves; and, in all probability, an appealing ignorance of Soviet nuclear capabilities that they were trying to balance with our own.

If there are any hopes for negotiating at all realistically in the future, we must, at a minimum, fill our void of ignorance regarding Soviet nuclear capabilities. This would call for the United States producing an updated version of Dwight Eisenhower's open-skies proposal, where aerial inspection would have to be brought down to earth in the Soviet Union. Cameras, electronic surveillance, what have you, in orbit, which readily can be deceived by the Soviets, whose military doctrine holds deception as a cardinal tenet, will have to be replaced by U.S. technical personnel on Soviet terra firma. These personnel would have unlimited access to every nook and cranny of the USSR where nuclear-weapon facilities are known or suspected to exist. At the same time, of course, the Soviets would have identical access to our facilities.

Such an arrangement would, in effect, establish on both sides an organization of "legal spies" who would have the essential responsibility of providing for their countries data which could form the basis for sound arms-control negotiations. If both sides genuinely wish to reduce the risk of nuclear war by constraining and reducing each other's nuclear arsenals through arms control, a prerequisite for such action has to include an understanding of each other's arsenals. This can be obtained only through unlimited inspection.*

To negotiate nuclear-weapons treaties in the absence of such understanding, and to attempt to enforce the treaties through space-based verification means, is fallacious and perilous, regardless of how accurate the verification process may be. This is putting

---

* During the initial phase of the SALT I discussions, our delegation explained the logical necessity for both sides to know the size of each other's nuclear arsenals. We naturally told the Russians about our arsenal, expecting them to reciprocate. But they couldn't because, so they claimed, they simply didn't know. Since this presented a problem, at least to us, our delegation sought permission from Washington to tell the Russians what size arsenal they had. Washington consented and the Russians found out what they had. Of course, the agreement that was reached via SALT I had nothing to do with those data. It amounted to little more than the Russians agreeing not to deploy more missiles than we told them what we thought they had. Incredible, but true.

the cart before the horse; it is pointless to engage in verifying treaties that were unsound and most probably inimical to our national security in the first place. To go on seeking treaties enforced through verification is little more than legitimatizing a process for our downfall.

Were the United States to consider moving in the direction of what we might call an open-nations proposal for negotiating treaties, this would produce one of the most agonizing moments of truth imaginable for our government. For this would amount to a candid admission to the American people that our intelligence on Soviet nuclear capabilities may have been grossly deficient. The government, in essence, would be confessing that it may not have been realistically and safely pursuing nuclear arms control. It would be an admission that the U.S. intelligence community may have deceived itself and the government, or had been politically pressured by the government, or both, into believing that almost everything it had seen of Soviet nuclear-weapon capabilities was almost everything that existed.

Large bureaucratic organizations (of which the U.S. intelligence community is one) always have been loath to admit serious faults and thereby risk the wrath of budget cutters. There are thousands of people in industry and government connected with producing and operating these technically dazzling spy satellites, while expending billions of dollars each year, having powerful backing in the Congress and the U.S. arms-control community. What can be predicted with confidence is that were the intelligence community to be pressed to justify its technical monitoring capabilities for determining the nature and extent of Soviet nuclear capabilities, the reaction, reflecting its organizational belief (or survival instinct), would go something like this: "It would be too risky for the Soviets to attempt to hide their nuclear weapons on any large scale. Surely, with so many people involved in such a massive enterprise, word would sooner or later leak out. Surely, sooner or later, there would be a slip-up in such a huge concealment program and our spy satellites would see at least one instance of what they were up to. And since we haven't seen such an instance [although it's possible that we have but, as we have done before on matters of arms-control violations, were unwilling to rock the boat over such a 'small' bit of evidence, in light of the political furor that might arise], we have no grounds for suspecting them of such perfidy."

There have been rumors of hidden nuclear missile installations in the USSR, but, assuming we tried seriously to check on them, apparently nothing was uncovered. There have been reports over many years of huge Soviet installations, with whole towns supporting them, but the problem is that we have not been able to look inside them. All we could do was to speculate, inconclusively, what was under cover. Considering the great military logic for the Soviets' attempting to conceal their true nuclear capabilities from U.S. nuclear targeting analysts, we should long ago have paid serious attention to an article in a Soviet General Staff journal in the early 1970s we managed to get our hands on; the article stated:

> If it is not possible to conceal troops and facilities from hostile observation, then one can reduce their revealing features by altering their external appearance. For example, a large camp or supply base can be camouflaged as a town; a tank farm can be camouflaged as apartment houses, while individual military installations can be camouflaged as rubble, smoldering ruins, etc. Such action can be employed not only at the tactical echelon but particularly at . . . strategic levels.

We should keep in mind that the great bulk of the vast USSR land mass is closed not only to foreign visitors and diplomatic personnel, but also to the Soviet citizenry. Even the Soviet military is tightly compartmentalized, and access to military information is restricted in accordance with specific duties. The USSR is a closed society in every sense of the word. Secrecy has taken on the most unbelievable dimensions, which we in the West might regard as paranoidal, but which the Soviets regard as crucial for preserving their security.

In this sense, one easily can imagine the Soviets constructing a nuclear missile base camouflaged as a town having some industry (say, lumbering or light manufacturing), with nearby farming areas, with the requisite number of sheds and warehouses (containing the missiles and their auxiliary equipment); all of this constituting enough activity to require a rail spur and regular rail traffic—to supply and maintain the base. To guarantee secrecy further (as I witnessed when I was stationed at Los Alamos during World War II), the townspeople not directly engaged in operating and maintaining the missiles, could easily be insulated from the weapon facilities, or even be misinformed on what was going on. Military equipment and personnel could arrive on base at night to avoid observation (not only from the townspeople but also from our spy satellites, in case we began getting suspicious), whereas innocuous items (cars, trucks, farm and industrial equipment, supplies, what have you) could be delivered during the day for all to see, including our satellites.

In 1974 the Soviet defense minister, Marshal Andrei Grechko, expressed his dismay over the refusal of the U.S. and other Western countries to accept the official declaratory Soviet military doctrine:

> Soviet military doctrine is attracting great attention in capitalist countries. A great number of books and articles are published on this theme and many lectures read. Some of the authors, falsifying events and facts, try to discredit Soviet military doctrine, to form a false opinion about it.
>
> We have never hidden and are not hiding the basic principal positions of our military doctrine. They are expressed with utmost clarity in the policies of the Communist Party and the Soviet government, in the state of our armed forces.[1]

Here was the foremost military figure in the USSR, a powerful member of the Politburo, stating flatly that Soviet military doctrine clearly reflected the basic policy of the USSR and practically pleading with us to accept the fact that they really meant what they were saying.

As remarked earlier, the most important doctrinal tenet, stressed repeatedly in their official military literature, is the element of surprise. Soviet military textbooks and encyclopedias emphasize the need to surprise the enemy, particularly in the context of nuclear war. Surprise is achieved mainly "as a result of poor knowledge by the adversary of one's true intentions, as a result of subjective errors in assessing intentions and plans, as well as a result of shallow analyses of measures taken to achieve surprise." Which couldn't depict better how the United States, in approaching nuclear arms control, has so willingly fallen into the Soviet trap that the Soviets made perfectly clear they were setting.

On one hand, we chose to believe the Soviets' external propaganda that enunciated their dedication to nuclear arms control. On the other hand, however, we refused to believe that they weren't about to give us a clear picture of what they were up to in nuclear arms, even though they had made it clear that they weren't. In other words, we chose to go along with Soviet lies, because they sounded so awfully nice; but we refused to go along with their avowed truths because they were just too painful.

Lenin once instructed his disciples on how to deal with the capitalists: "Tell them what they want to hear." When it comes to nuclear arms control, his Soviet disciples have really followed their master's orders; and the American capitalists just can't hear enough.

Let's suppose a miracle were to happen in the U.S. government: it finally decided to come clean and admit to itself and to the American people that little confidence was to be had in our nuclear intelligence assessment of the Russians. As a consequence, little confidence should be placed in the credibility of past nuclear arms-control agreements, in particular the two SALT accords. No longer should we be bound by them.

With this miracle in hand, the United States should now propose to the Russians that either they accept full inspection before negotiating another agreement or there will be no more negotiations. In effect, we would be telling them: "Look, you fellows have been right all along on your openly announced policy of deception and disinformation. We've been foolish enough in the past not to have taken you at your word on how you've been striving to mislead us. We may have called you a bunch of deceitful thugs running an 'evil empire' but we were certain that you really believed in nuclear arms control and that you would never mislead us on so critical a matter. But by gosh, we were wrong about your being right about yourselves. All's fair in love and nuclear war, and we now accept your avowals that you actually have been adhering to your policy and beguiling the breeches off us. However, if you really are sincere about nuclear arms control, as you've claimed you are, then you'll have to cut out all this secrecy and let us in to see how sincere you've been. And we'll let you into our country to prove our sincerity. How about it?"

Now virtually all of us would put the odds at a thousand to one against the Russians accepting our proposal. Since they've always been willing to talk with us, while building up and up their nuclear arsenal, chances are they would denounce so dastardly an accusation—but then suggest that we talk this over in a reasonable way, while they continued to build.

On the other hand, it always has been the Soviets' policy to avoid unduly risky undertakings in their march to world domination. And nuclear war under any conditions has to be a pretty risky business. Their game plan so far has been to advance through subversion (as they've been doing in Latin America) and use military surrogates (as they've been doing practically everywhere). So maybe a thousand to one is a bit high; but whatever the odds might actually be, let's suppose that to reduce the risk of nuclear war they said: "Okay. It's a deal. Come on over with your inspectors." Would we then say: "Hallelujah! Peace at last!" Maybe not. For we might discover after poking around that the "definite margin of superiority" President Reagan has conceded to them is actually a *decisive* margin.

Suppose we found out that the Soviets had stashed away far larger numbers of ICBMs than we thought they would under the SALT constraints. Suppose, upon closely examining their Backfire bombers, it turned out that they had intercontinental capabilities all along; and the same held true for the SS-20s. Also, suppose we were able to confirm our suspicions over their air-defense missiles having ABM capabilities; that certain nuclear development sites were testing advanced ABM concepts, such as particle beam weapons, and considerable progress had been made. Finally, suppose we discovered that their civil defense system and industrial protection program were much more extensive than we had led ourselves to believe.

If all this were revealed to us, because the Soviets, for their reasons, were willing to let us find out what they had accomplished, what would our reaction be? You know darned well what it would be: shock and horror. Suddenly, we would realize that we were so far behind that our options for dealing with the Soviets were extremely limited—especially in conducting nuclear arms-control negotiations. With the Soviets now so decisively in the driver's seat, what could we do except hope that our nuclear deterrent against direct attack on the United States still had credence? And then commence to do (in a frenzy) what we should have been doing all along: build up our defenses against nuclear attack.

So maybe, despite all the logic behind the case for full inspection to precede nuclear arms-control talks, we might not want to pick up a Soviet offer to allow such inspection, for fear of what we might find. And keep in mind that were the Soviets not to have a demonstrably decisive nuclear advantage over us, there's little chance that, unless really willing to go all out for nuclear disarmament, they would invite us in to find out. In either case, however, whether they let us in or kept us out, the case for continuing with nuclear arms-control negotiations is pretty difficult to justify. The problem is, we have let too much time go by on the issue of inspection, while we dilly-dallied and hoped and prayed that arms control could be made to work. As a result, we may have reached the time when it no longer can work because it simply isn't workable. We've allowed the situation to get too far out of control by being so naive—and damned stupid.

All this having been said, I feel that it still would be in our best interests to make a proposal for full, open inspection to the Russians. For unless we do this we will continue traipsing down the primrose path into an increasingly insecure future. If there are any realistic prospects for nuclear arms control, they must be founded on facts and truths, not on hopes and unfounded assumptions.

It would be nice if we could start all over again, with our initial ideals for controlling the Bomb, but with our initial hardboiled attitude for enforcing such control through unlimited inspection. However, the clock can't be turned back and if the Soviets are genuinely interested in reducing the risk of nuclear war through arms control, they should be willing to reveal their true nuclear capabilities to us. If they are not willing, the only safe conclusion that can be reached by us is that they have accepted such risk as a reality of the nuclear age, despite their recent propaganda to the contrary.

In this event, it becomes imperative for us to move away from arms control and do our own thing in our own supreme national interests: taking realistic measures to avoid nuclear war by being able to defend ourselves against nuclear attack. This means spending our defense money to *defend* ourselves back here in the USA, instead of spending it on defending virtually everybody else around the world, a posture that holds the greatest risk of igniting a nuclear war.

Can nuclear arms control reduce the risk of nuclear war? I doubt it very much, because I very much doubt that the Soviets have ever shared our views on the matter. Instead, they have viewed arms control as an effective means of reducing the risks to their survival, while increasing ours. One way or another, however, we should force this issue to a head by forcing a resolution of the inspection issue, which we should have done at the very beginning.

5

Can We Avoid Nuclear War and *The Day After?*

ONE OF THE MOST FRUITLESS things a person can do is to discuss the Vietnam war with those who held responsibilities for getting us into it or fighting it. Many of those involved in the policy planning that led to our involvement will complain that the military planners had given them false estimates of the situation. But many military planners will complain that the policy planners, their civilian superiors, unduly straitjacketed military operations, which their original estimates did not take into account. For example, had they been allowed to take the war into North Vietnam from the very beginning, the frustrations of fighting in the South Vietnamese jungles and swamps could mainly have been avoided and the war won in short order.

Getting back to the policy types, they usually will argue that South Vietnam was a formal ally of ours and for us not to have come to its defense would have had disastrous effects on other allies, who otherwise might have sought accommodation with the communists. This supposedly would have been disastrous for us—economically, politically, and militarily. And many of the policy types will argue that had they not confined the U.S. ground forces to the South, the Red Chinese might have jumped in (as in the Korean war) and then we really would have had a mess on our hands, one perhaps forcing us to use nuclear weapons and risking escalation to all-out nuclear war, and all that. Without a doubt, fear of nuclear escalation (of the kind that took place in *The Day After*) had a profound effect on our deportment in the Vietnam war; and thereby on its outcome, which included our defeat. In no small way did our desire to avoid nuclear war, in planning our policy for the Vietnam war, lead to our losing the war.

However, as mentioned above, the rehashing and blame-calling are fruitless, solving nothing. The plain unhappy fact of the matter is that our policies and military strategy governing the conduct of that war did not allow us to win it. As a result, the American patience and tolerance ran out and we were forced to pull out; which, in effect, constituted a defeat. That being the case, a fair question (based on the unfair advantage of hindsight) to be asked is: Why did we get into that war; what were our objectives?

I'm afraid that there are no clear answers to the question (no more so than for our recent military involvement in Lebanon). Looking back at our national security policy at that time, we can see that the only policy objective that seemed to dictate our Vietnam involvement was the containment of communism through a series of military alliances around the world. That was the essence of our foreign policy; it still is. However, *containment*, by itself, not only is a difficult concept to defend, it having no positive aspects, but also runs against the grain of national behavior and the history of nations, especially communist nations. Holding to such a military concept for the defense of our allies, we can only lose; the question being: How much? For the case of Vietnam, the answer is: about everything—an enormous amount of money; a tragic toll in American soldiers killed and wounded; a deep divisiveness in our society; and, what our containment policy forbade us to lose, the loss of an ally's freedom. To repeat, however, overshadowing these tragic losses was our great and understandable desire to avoid nuclear war. That should have taught us an invaluble lesson: the best way to avoid such tragedies as Vietnam, and to avoid risking nuclear war, is to avoid getting into such predicaments in the first place—namely, avoid getting into foreign wars. Very briefly, toward the end of our Vietnam involvement and for a few years later, it appeared that we had learned that lesson.

Upon becoming president, Richard Nixon took stock of the wretched situation in Southeast Asia and the soured American mood on foreign military interventions, and set about formulating a new U.S. policy for containing communism in Asia, in which we would assist our Asian allies by providing military material but not U.S. military forces. This new policy, outlined by the president in the summer of 1969, became known as the Nixon doctrine and was hailed as the showpiece of his administration's foreign policy.

In his 1971 report to the Congress, Nixon made it clear that the new U.S. intentions for supporting Asian allies would never again entail dispatching American armies to foreign shores to fight conventional wars: ". . . we shall furnish military and economic assistance when requested in accordance with our treaty commitments. But we shall look to the nation directly threatened to assume the primary responsibility for providing the manpower for its defense." He also made it clear that America no longer would retain the mantle of world policeman:

> We will continue to provide elements of military strength and economic resources appropriate to our size and our interests. But it is no longer natural or possible in this age to argue that security or development around the globe is primarily America's concern. The defense and progress of other countries must be first their responsibility and second a regional responsibility. Without the foundations of self-help and regional help, American help will not succeed.

No doubt about it, according to President Nixon, there would be no more U.S. land wars in Asia. After the Vietnam fiasco, enough was enough.

Although the above remarks by Nixon were made in an Asian context, they could as well have been applied to our NATO alliance in Europe. In fact, polls taken around that time showed a sizable erosion of American support for defending Europe with U.S. troops. However, as for the Asian situation, the erosion was almost entirely emotional and had little to do with the military facts surrounding NATO and the danger of nuclear war in the event of another war in Europe, a danger far greater than that of another Asian war involving our forces (which *The Day After* could have brought out to the American people, had the movie been made at that time).

Even before the Vietnam war and its agonies were over, the miserable episode began to fade rapidly from the American mind. Once our forces were withdrawn from South Vietnam, whatever "lessons" we had learned from the war—the lessons that brought about the Nixon doctrine—seemed forgotten. Before you knew it the United States was acting as though the war and the Nixon

85

doctrine never had existed. For example, in March 1974 the secretary of defense, James Schlesinger, in his report to the Congress, was warning that even though the war had produced "major changes" in our Asian policies, "Nevertheless, we consider the possibility of conflict in Asia in deciding upon the characteristics and forward deployment of United States forces, because the continuing instabilities in Asia could involve the United States, and because having the visible capabilities to act can help to avoid, through deterrence, the necessity for action." In other words, our policy once again called for U.S. military intervention in another Asian war, completely contrary to the Nixon doctrine. Needless to say, the secretary's report did not even give lip service to the short-lived policy; in fact, it was not even mentioned by name.

Very early in his term, President Jimmy Carter gave the impression that he remembered the Nixon doctrine, when he sought to withdraw U.S. ground forces from South Korea. However, his efforts to accomplish this end ran into a storm of public denunciation and the Congress forbade him to make any significant withdrawals. And when the Soviets invaded Afghanistan in late 1979, the Carter administration became downright hawkish in its military commitments to Asia, setting up the Rapid Deployment Force designed primarily for coping with the threat of a Soviet invasion in the Persian Gulf region, but also for deployment to other Asian regions if the need arose.

In 1980 presidential candidate Ronald Reagan made it clear that his position on the U.S. military role in Asia had nothing in common with the Nixon doctrine. The Republican platform proposed to the convention in July (to which Reagan pledged himself) stated: "A new Republican administration will restore a strong military role in Asia and the Pacific. We will make it clear that any military action which threatens the independence of America's allies and friends will bring a response sufficient to make its cost prohibitive to potential adversaries."

This was one promise that Reagan set about keeping as soon as he became president, as reflected by a statement on Asian defense commitments made in April 1981 by his defense secretary, Caspar Weinberger: "We are prepared to help defend our friends and our allies, and to deter aggression, and we are determined to be a reliable and a strong ally. An important corollary to that is the expectation that we have that our allies and friends in Asia and elsewhere will participate in meeting our common security interests." That was the sort of language one heard coming from Wash-

86

ington before our going to war in Vietnam, and the opposite of what the Nixon doctrine had in mind for our role in Asian wars.

Why in the world have the American people and their elected representatives in the Congress allowed the Nixon doctrine, so widely applauded at the time of its inception, to suffer such an ignominious demise? Why have their memories of the terrible trauma that brought it about been so unbelievably short? I don't profess to know the answers to these questions, which most Americans seem not to have asked of themselves. I can only refer back to the discussion in Chapter 1, and Hilaire Belloc's "large and awful faces from beyond" who watch over us; and repeat that this reflects "the most dangerous and irrational form of behavior a nation can take."

About four years ago, I was interviewed for a national security position by a high-ranking administration official. The official had a very distinguished background in foreign policy and was a re- nowned expert in international law. At one point in our discussion he stated very dramatically that the world had become a jungle where the revered principles of international law had largely been discarded. I emphatically agreed with him and then proceeded (not too wisely, I guess) to tell him that we (the United States) ought to get out of that jungle as fast as we can, to avoid nuclear war. Whereupon he froze; that was the end of the interview—and my chances for a job.

For all the reasons brought out earlier here, if we really do want to avoid nuclear war and be able to survive the perils of the nuclear age, we had better part company with our military interventionist policies and apply the Nixon doctrine outside our hemisphere, and reassert the Monroe Doctrine to prevent Soviet intrusion into our hemisphere.

In no sense of the word am I suggesting that we precipitately abandon our friends and allies around the world and leave them vulnerable to communist aggression; or, knowing that they are vulnerable, to political blackmail and intimidation. Rather, as the Nixon doctrine called for, if they really want to defend themselves (and in most cases they can), we should furnish them with the military tools realistically required for their defense, which in some cases would have to include nuclear weapons. But if we want to avoid nuclear war, which has to be our paramount national objec- tive, we can't go on holding to the myth that we can keep the free world from Soviet enslavement by dispatching conventional armies to foreign shores. To the contrary, by continuing with this myth we are practically guaranteeing that sooner or later we'll get into a war with the Soviets that will become a strategic nuclear war. And if this dreaded event found us absolutely defenseless against nuclear attack, as we now are and will be into the foreseeable future, that would be the end of our freedom, to say nothing of the horrible toll in American lives and suffering.

Never before in our nation's history has this assessment of our primary national security objective, preserving our liberty, had more meaning than today, when, for the first time in our nation's history, our liberty is directly threatened by the possibility of nuclear war. The time has come—in fact, is overdue—when the United States must move away from its self-assumed responsibility for defending others from Soviet attack, for which purpose most of our defense moneys now go, and turn to its own terribly neglected defenses, to be able to survive.

Early in 1984, writing in the *Wall Street Journal*, Jay Winick, executive director of the Coalition for a Democratic Majority, admonished the left wing of his party for its resistance to the U.S. containment policy. He expressed concern that the Left may once again dominate Democratic foreign policy thinking and thereby ruin the chances of the Democrats for taking over the White House. Said Winick:

> The logic of the Democratic Left is fallacious and irresponsible. It ignores the fact that as the senior partner of NATO and the most powerful democratic nation, the U.S. has vital security interests in its commitments abroad, as well as a moral responsibility to uphold them. At times, these commitments will necessitate the use of force, and even sacrifices in the blood and treasure of young Americans. And for U.S. diplomatic efforts to be credible, an imperative in the nuclear age, they must be backed up by an adequate defense establishment.
>
> Should the Democrats fall under the spell of the Left once again, then the majority party will be consigned to another four years of watching a Republican president appeal more to the Democratic Party's natural constituency than it does. More than just an opportunity for the White House will have been squandered. At just the time when the Democratic Party finally seems to be responding to the true profile of its supporters, it may risk splintering in much the same way as did the British Labor Party.

Heaven only knows that, as an inveterate nuclear hawk with a record of favoring the strongest possible nuclear defenses for our country, my sympathies for the views of the Democratic Left have been very few and far between. I have held their views to be mainly fallacious, irresponsible, and dangerous; and still do on most national security issues, especially nuclear issues. However, when I see such attacks against them as Winick's, I'm almost tempted to come to their side; for such attacks are about as devoid of logic and responsibility regarding our vital security interests as they can be. They represent a blind defense of a policy that once may have been in our vital interests but now has become dangerous to our vital interests, because it holds an intolerable risk of nuclear war.

The real moral responsibility that should underlie our national security policies is the moral imperative to protect the United States, not the protection of other countries. If we continue to adhere to our policy of military intervention abroad, based on conventional forces, this will be tantamount to not being able to protect anybody—our friends and allies, or ourselves. Whatever the fate of our friends and allies may be if we force them to decide on their own defense, we would hope that they survive and should provide them with the military equipment necessary for their survival that they cannot provide for themselves. But our foremost policy requirement is that the United States be in a position to survive and carry on as a free democratic institution, which we are least likely to do if we go on spending most of our defense money for fighting foreign wars.

During 1787–88 three Founding Fathers—Alexander Hamilton, James Madison, and John Jay—wrote *The Federalist*, a series of essays on the proposed U.S. Constitution and on the nature of representative government. Regarding the prime objective for our country, *The Federalist* stated: "Among the many objects to which a wise and free people find it necessary to direct their attention, that of providing for their safety seems to be the first." To provide best for our safety in the nuclear age, two fundamental objectives must be met: (1) avoiding involvement in wars that may become a nuclear war; and (2) being able to protect ourselves against nuclear attack and thereby demonstrating to the attacker that his strategy will not succeed, so that he will not attack. Having practically exhaustively discussed how to meet the first objective, we shall now turn to meeting the second.

Let's suppose that sometime tomorrow the Soviets were to

launch a surprise nuclear attack on the United States. By the U.S. government's own admission and using data that it dutifully releases to the American people (who mainly shirk their duties as responsible citizens and pay no attention whatsoever), this would result in the destruction of perhaps 90 percent of our Minuteman ICBMs, about two thirds of our B-52 bomber forces, and about half of our nuclear missile submarines. In addition, very little of the command, control, and communications system, by which the president (if he were still alive) could direct nuclear operations, would be left. Moreover, most of our bases containing military forces that could resist a threatened Soviet invasion would have been destroyed. Finally, it would be evident that the Soviets had gone out of their way, in accordance with their stated doctrine for fighting a nuclear war, to avoid damaging U.S. towns and cities. Faced with this situation, what could the president do? Very little, I'm afraid, unless he chose to retaliate by attacking the Soviet civilian sector—and killing millions of noncombatants and destroying as much as possible of their economy—all in all, a grossly immoral act.

He would be in no position to fight a nuclear war with the Russians, for all the reasons previously brought out. Even if he tried to fight such a war, he would be faced with prolonging the agonies (depicted in *The Day After*) of an American people almost completely exposed to the effects of nuclear explosions because their government had not provided them with civil defense or defense against missile and bombing attacks. To all intents and purposes, the president would be faced with the problem of already having lost the military war and the moral issue of wreaking revenge by killing Soviet innocents, while American innocents were being killed. What sense would that make?

The answer has to be, of course, none. But not to worry, the president would say, as his predecessors have said, for this problem will never arise; the Russians will never attack. As everybody knows (except maybe the Russians), they are deterred from doing this by U.S. fiat; nuclear war will be so horrible that no Soviet leader in his right mind will ever contemplate making such an attack. And the U.S. threat to retaliate against the Russian attack, however irrational and immoral it may be, is quite sufficient to deter the attack. As President Reagan has said time after time, nobody can win a nuclear war. So why would the Russians start a war they could only lose?

We've discussed this question already and the answer seems to have been given long ago by the Russians, when they set about preparing to fight and win a nuclear war, and survive as a viable society still under communist control. For any American, including the president, to decide for the Russians that they have undertaken this enormous effort (while the Soviet economy has been allowed to suffer greatly) all in vain has to be presumptuous to an extreme. And dangerous as well, for this kind of self-deception has led to a self-blinding to what the Soviets actually have been up to. We have been unwilling to look objectively at Soviet efforts to survive nuclear war, in no small way for fear that we might find out that they might be able to survive.

Take, for example, the issue of Soviet civil defense and the extent of their program in this area. Despite consistent reports over many years by defectors and émigrés, our intelligence, for the reasons just given, has refused to make a purposeful attempt to determine the scope of the Soviet civil defense program. It wasn't until analyses performed outside the government led to pressures on the government that a serious review of the existing data took place; and then the widespread existence of urban shelters, relocation sites, and even some duplicate industrial facilities began to emerge. Even then, the CIA, for the same reasons it hadn't looked very hard for the data, managed to find it not convincing enough to warrant any real concern over the possibility of Soviet survival.

Without going into the flaws of the CIA study, which were plenty, I would make the observation that the only group that could have made a thoroughly objective assessment of Soviet civil defense would be a Soviet group; only such a group would have full access to all the relevant data. One would presume, of course, that such a group did in fact exist and found that civil defense could be an effective element of the Soviet strategy for surviving nuclear war.

Now I'm not trying to say that tomorrow, or the day after, or a month or a year after, the Soviets, based on an exhaustive analysis of their capabilities and ours (what they call a "correlation of forces"), will have arrived at the conclusion that they can successfully pull off a surprise nuclear attack—and then make the decision to do it. Rather, what I am saying is that nobody can logically rule out that possibility; for the logic behind such a Soviet decision has to be *their* logic, based on their stated objective, which is the imposition of communism on the world. To be sure, the Soviets have always preferred to accomplish their goals through means other than military conquest; and in the nuclear age their preference certainly has been sharpened greatly. In this respect, one notes the extreme caution the Soviets have displayed to date on getting into military conflicts with the West, choosing instead to pursue their aims through subversion and terrorism. However, this never has precluded the military option, including nuclear weapons. And only the Soviets can decide on this option and the risks involved.

In this context, for the United States to continue to base its nuclear strategy solely on the hope that deterrence, as we have gone about it, somehow will always manage to work has to be absolutely intolerable to the majority of the American people, who have never really accepted such a situation and have always expressed their desire for defense against nuclear attack. The trouble has been that each time an administration has attempted to provide such defense, the antinuclear factions in the country—especially those in the media and those having great influence on the media—have put up a tremendous howl of protest and denunciation. This has resulted in political pressures on the Congress, which in turn applies them to the White House; and the president backs away. The majority of the American people are left bewildered over why a president, supposedly in possession of all the relevant facts, would rather yield to the politics of the issue than squarely face up to it, which he seemed to be doing in the first place.

If one judges the profundity of a scientist by the amount of media exposure he gets (and gets for himself), then Carl Sagan (who more than anyone else has brought the cosmos before the American people) has to be the most profound scientist alive. Over the last eighteen months—on national television, in national weekly news-magazines, in Sunday supplement magazines like *Parade*, and in major newspapers—millions of Americans have been exposed to Sagan's accounting of the end of the world via nuclear war. Although past scientific investigations had not arrived at such hope-less conclusions, the work of Sagan and his colleagues showed that one of the effects of nuclear war had not been fully analyzed in the past. This was the tremendous amount of smoke from urban conflagrations invading the atmosphere, which would blot out the sun to a degree where for many months the world would go through what Sagan called a "nuclear winter." Temperatures on the earth's surface would plummet to subzero levels and the obscuration of the sun would reduce light levels to a twilight gloom or worse. The effect on the environment and ecology could be disastrous.*

As if this global freeze weren't bad enough, Sagan presents estimates that maybe a billion people might be killed and a comparable number seriously injured from the immediate effects of a nuclear war in which most of the major cities in the Northern Hemisphere were bombed. The social disruption for the survivors would be almost incomprehensible, with no electricity, fuel, transportation, food deliveries, etc. This is practically ten times as bad as the estimates given a decade or more back when most "experts" were predicting a few hundred million or so casualties, where the city attacks were confined to a U.S.–USSR nuclear exchange. Which leads to the question: Where on earth did Sagan, whose business is the cosmos, not nuclear war, drum up these hideous results? Well it turns out that he didn't get these results from those professionally engaged in the nuclear-war business; instead, they came from a study conducted by the World Health Organization, which is not renowned for its expertise on matters of nuclear strategy, nuclear weapons, and the nature of nuclear conflict.

What emerges when one examines the claims of Carl Sagan (or those of Jonathan Schell in his bestselling book *The Fate of the Earth*) is that both the U.S. and the USSR seem to have a nuclear strategy, which is to be implemented by extremely powerful nuclear warheads, and which includes the intention of bombing virtually every major city on each side. In this respect, you may recall that in *The Day After*, Kansas City was bombed into oblivion by the Soviets. How accurately does this represent the facts of the matter?

On the Soviet side, if one examines the military doctrine that underlies the state objectives, which are *political* objectives for waging nuclear war, there is no evidence that attacks on the enemy's cities are planned. To the contrary, the Soviets intend to avoid such devastation and carnage. After all, their primary objective always has been the communization of the "exploited masses" in the capitalist countries, not their liquidation, which is reserved for the

*Sagan has stated that Soviet scientists have made independent assessments of this frigid aftermath and basically confirmed his findings. However, when Soviets scientists have been asked for their papers on this subject, the only paper forthcoming was based on the U.S. research. When a vice president of the USSR Academy of Sciences, Yevgeniy P. Velikhov (believed to be a member of the KGB), was asked by U.S. Sovietologist Leon Gouré why Soviet scientists have not cited their own independent assessments, his answer was: "We use your data; we just interpret it our way."

capitalist rulers. In this regard, if one examines the nature of Soviet nuclear doctrine during its formative years, it is seen that the broad guidance given by the Soviet high command, the General Staff, is in the direction of fighting a nuclear war for *military* purposes, to bring about a military defeat of the enemy. To illustrate this point, here are some statements from articles that appeared during the 1960s (when the Soviet nuclear missile force was building up) in *Military Thought,* the official journal of the General Staff:

> Theses of Soviet military strategy primarily reflect the political strategy of the Communist Party of the Soviet Union. It is in the interests of political strategy that military strategy makes use of the achievements of scientific-technical progress which materializes in weapons of varying power . . . [certain weapons can] lead to defeat of the enemy's armed forces without doing essential injury to the economy or populace of states whose aggressive rulers unleashed the war. Only political leadership can determine the scale and consistency of bringing to bear the most powerful means of destruction.

> The objective is not to turn the large economic and industrial regions into a heap of ruins . . . but to deliver strikes which will destroy strategic combat means, paralyze enemy military production, making it incapable of satisfying the priority needs of the front and rear areas and sharply reduce the enemy capability to conduct strikes.

> Initial attention is given to the selection of those enemy targets against which nuclear means could be used. Depending on the features of the strike targets, a selection is made of the nuclear weapons carriers . . . which could best and most rapidly execute the assigned mission with minimum expenditure of explosive power.

Perhaps the one fly in the ointment in the above statements is the amount of urban destruction (including fires that might produce the dreaded "nuclear winter") resulting from the attack on military production targets, which frequently are in or near major U.S. cities. On this issue, two observations are in order.

First, it is noted that the objective in attacking such targets is to "paralyze" their operation, which does not necessarily imply their destruction. In this connection, since the Soviets have not been inhibited against the use of chemical and biological weapons, which are nondestructive and need not even be lethal, it is entirely possible, even highly probable, that these weapons have been earmarked for use against militarily related targets in and around urban areas. (Again, such use would be in accordance with stated political objectives.) As of now and into the foreseeable future,

American industry, war-related or other, is vulnerable to chemical and biological attacks. As such, there would be a compelling logic for the Soviets to make such attacks.

Second, even were the Soviets to decide on attacking such targets with nuclear weapons, by no means does this imply that they would employ highly destructive weapons. Not only would this run contrary to their declared nuclear doctrine, but, if they believed in the possibility of a "nuclear winter" being produced by such attacks, they would be doubly defeating their purposes. Not only would they have deprived themselves of gaining an intact U.S. economy for their exploitation; they would have succeeded in wrecking their own economy by putting their country into a deep freeze.

According to U.S. intelligence estimates, Soviet missile accuracies have become about as good as ours, which are pretty darned good; we're able to get warheads within several hundred feet of ground zero. On this basis, were nuclear weapons to be used against U.S. production facilities, explosive powers of but a thousandth (or even less) of those popularly ascribed to the Soviet strategic nuclear arsenal would more than suffice to paralyze operation of these facilities. However, since this still would run against the Soviets' objectives, what they might really have in mind here (if they were hell-bent on using nuclear weapons) is using neutron warheads, which would neutralize the work force while leaving the plant intact. The Soviets claim to have successfully developed neutron weapons many years ago, and maybe this was one of the applications they had in mind.

From such considerations, one wonders where Carl Sagan and others of his ilk got information on the Soviet nuclear attack strategy which allowed them to calculate such apocalyptic consequences. They certainly couldn't have obtained it from the Soviets. In fact, even if the Soviets actually had such a diabolical plan for the incineration of U.S. cities, they certainly wouldn't have so informed Sagan, in effect telling him that in waging nuclear war against the United States they intended to terminate themselves and civilization as well. And yet the Sagans and such antinuclear groups as the World Health Organization, aided and abetted by the Soviets, who are more than happy to see the U.S. lose confidence in defending itself against nuclear attack, go on merrily perpetrating what may be little more than a hoax. But a dangerous hoax regarding the survival of the U.S. and other Western nations. And worst of all, the U.S. government, which has been mainly responsible for the public release of official Soviet military thinking (which is confirmed by highly classified documents that have fallen into our hands, that haven't been released publicly), has for political reasons been paralyzed in exposing this hoax.

During the 1950s and 1960s U.S. nuclear strategy, to be sure, was based heavily on deliberate attacks on Soviet cities and their inhabitants. During the 1970s, however, this began to change and policies were established holding to strategies not too different from those that had been adopted by the Russians. At present, U.S. policy explicitly rejects such attacks, as evidenced by Defense Secretary Weinberger's statement in 1983:

> Yet, some believe that we must threaten explicitly, even solely, the mass destruction of civilians on the adversary side, thus inviting a corresponding destruction of civilian populations on our side, and that such a posture will achieve stability in deterrence. This is incorrect. Such a threat is neither moral nor prudent. The Reagan administration's policy is that under no circumstances may such weapons be used deliberately for the purpose of destroying populations.
>
> For this reason, we disagree with those who hold that deterrence should be based on nuclear weapons designed to destroy cities rather than military targets. Deliberately designing weapons aimed at populations is neither necessary nor sufficient for deterrence. If we are forced to retaliate and can only respond by destroying population centers, we invite the destruction of our own population. . . .

This statement would seem to belie the nuclear-war scenarios that Carl Sagan embraces to enable predicting the end of practically everything, but the trouble is, in the list of targets that the new policy holds to, there are many which are in or next to major cities. These are a series of targets related to postwar Soviet economic recuperation which we would like to destroy to make sure that (as Strangelovian as this may sound) the Russians will not emerge in a better postwar situation than ourselves.

The United States has rejected the use of chemical and biological weapons for strategic purposes and has not sought to minimize its nuclear-warhead yields in accordance with requirements stemming from the discriminate attack of economic targets, so the current and currently planned stockpile of strategic nuclear warheads in effect provides grist for Sagan's nuclear incineration mill. Which, if Sagan's calculations are even halfway accurate, means that this component of our strategy is badly lacking in credibility. Were nuclear war to start, only an insane U.S. president would direct such attacks to be made. Assuming that no president would be that insane, then one can only assume that the U.S. contribution to the "nuclear winter" produced by the burning of cities would not be made.

Another global life-destroying effect that Sagan and others have brought up is the massive irradiation of the earth's surface in the Northern Hemisphere by ultraviolet rays. This ostensibly will arise from the depletion of the ozone layer in the stratosphere caused by chemical reactions with clouds from high-yield nuclear explosions that rise into the ozone layer. It is the ozone layer that normally keeps the ultraviolet from seriously irradiating the surface; and in a nuclear war involving high-yield weapons, it has been calculated that this screen would substantially be destroyed. As Sagan has said:

> After a nuclear war in which thousands of high-yield weapons are detonated, the increase in biologically dangerous ultraviolet light might be several hundred percent. In the more dangerous shorter wave lengths, larger increases would occur. Nucleic acids and proteins, the fundamental molecules for life on earth, are especially sensitive to ultraviolet radiation. Thus, an increase of the solar ultraviolet flux at the surface of the Earth is potentially dangerous for life.[1]

The question here is: How likely is it that a nuclear war would involve thousands of high-yield weapons?

Although our knowledge of nuclear-produced ozone depletion is hardly precise, generally speaking, megaton yields or greater are required to push the clouds up into the ozone-layer level. What can be said about the Soviet stockpile and the number of such weapons they will detonate on U.S. targets? And, conversely, what can be said about our share of detonating such weapons?

On the Soviet side, one should realize that for over twenty years—since the signing of the Atmospheric Test Ban Treaty, which forced nuclear testing underground, thereby preventing U.S. analysis of debris from Soviet tests—we have not had hard evidence on the nature of Soviet testing. As a result, we have largely had to conjecture about what warheads the Soviets were developing for their strategic nuclear stockpile, in preparing intelligence estimates. In general, we have assumed that the Soviets were emplacing maximum-yield warheads (that is, the largest yield that could be fitted into their delivery payloads) in their strategic weapons. Those yields were determined by U.S. nuclear technology considerations, not those of the Soviets, which we did not know. Since the Soviets already had stated (in their military doctrinal writings) that they did not select *their* yields in that manner, our assumption very likely was wrong.

Furthermore, it is pointed out that those making such assumptions seem to have forgotten that a decade ago the Soviets entered into a treaty with the United States that prohibited testing of nuclear explosives above the 150-kiloton (0.15-megaton) level. This was the Threshold Test Ban Treaty (TTBT), whose importance was officially described by the U.S. Arms Control and Disarmament Agency thus:

> The Treaty on the Limitation of Underground Nuclear Weapons Tests, also known as the Threshold Test Ban Treaty (TTBT), was signed in July 1974. It establishes a nuclear "threshold," by prohibiting tests having a yield exceeding 150 kilotons (equivalent to 150,000 tons of TNT).
>
> The threshold is militarily important since it removes the possibility of testing new or existing nuclear weapons going beyond the fractional-megaton range. In the past decade, many tests above 150 kilotons have been conducted by both countries. The mutual restraint undertaken will significantly reduce the explosive force of new nuclear warheads and bombs which could otherwise be tested for weapons systems. . . .

New warhead developments usually consume a period of several years. On this basis, since the TTBT was signed, the Soviets may have completed two development cycles for their strategic warheads. In this context, the probability that they have retained megaton and multimegaton warheads in their arsenal would appear to be low. If this indeed is the situation, what can be reasonably assumed is that, in entering into the TTBT, the Soviets did so with the expectation that requirements for future warheads would not include high-yield warheads of the type that produce serious long-term global effects, such as ozone depletion.

Were civilization to be frozen and irradiated (with ultraviolet rays) to death by a nuclear war, to talk about defending the United States against nuclear attack to save the lives and social fabric of the American people would sound wildly irrational. Since it is far from clear, however, that civilization will be so imperiled as Sagan

98

and his cohorts make it out to be, maybe we ought to start giving more serious and objective attention to the survival of our country in the event of nuclear war. Or better yet, maybe we ought to start giving more serious and objective attention to being able to deter nuclear attack on us so that we can demonstrate to the Soviets that we can protect ourselves and survive; in other words, that they can't win. In realistically achieving this deterrent objective, let's begin with the issue of civil defense.

In 1982 a reputable polling organization (Sindlinger & Co.) was commissioned to survey U.S public opinion on civil defense. Here are two of the questions asked and the responses:

Do you believe that the U.S. government has a responsibility to provide an effective program of civil defense for all its citizens?

	All	Male	Female
Yes	81%	78%	85%
No	17	20	15
No opinion	2	2	1

Would you be willing to see the government allocate a greater proportion of its money for civil defense if this increase promised to significantly improve people's chances of survival in wartime?

	All	Male	Female
Yes	76%	71%	80%
No	21	27	16
No opinion	3	2	4

Plainly, the America people want to survive nuclear war, despite the insistence by a highly vocal minority, which manages to dominate the media and heavily influence the Congress with its propaganda that it is not survivable. Furthermore, they seem fully to expect, if not to demand, that their government do something about it. And they are more than willing to foot the bill if the government can advance a civil defense program that will improve their prospects for survival.

Obviously, something is wrong, terribly wrong, for to date the government, afraid to face up to the problem of surviving nuclear war and its domestic political consequences, has elected to yield to the antinuclear, anti-civil-defense minority and, in effect, to ignore the wishes of the majority. And even when it has tried to do something to help gain acceptance, it has done so in an extremely unrealistic and penny-pinching way; notwithstanding, it has failed to gain acceptance because of the political factor. Take, for example, the efforts of the Reagan administration in 1982 to establish a so-called crisis-relocation civil defense plan.

The plan was based on the expectation that there would be an international crisis (as in *The Day After*) preceding a nuclear war, supposedly giving enough time for urban residents to pack up, avoid traffic jams, evacuate their cities, and head for areas not expected to be directly attacked. Once there, preparations having been made in advance, fallout shelters would be constructed and stocked to enable the occupants to remain secure in the shelters until the fallout radiation level outside had died down to safe levels. Studies showed that such a plan, fully implemented, could reduce the number of civilian casualties by more than 80 percent from the level expected without such protection. One virtue of such a plan, intended to impress budget-minded congressmen, was its essential cheapness; a mere $4.3 billion was requested from the Congress to begin a program along these lines.

The result was disastrous. The bulk of the media, including its most powerful elements, heaped ridicule on the proposal. The Congress held hearings wherein administration officials, under intense political pressure, were forced to back away from their positions and confess that there was no way to survive an all-out nuclear attack on the United States; in effect, they joined ranks with the antinuclear opponents of civil defense. A leading Pentagon official sounded like Carl Sagan when he testified before a Senate committee: "We do not seek, nor do we believe that it is possible to obtain, levels of protection from the effects of all-out nuclear war that would reduce significantly the unspeakable horror of such an event." That gives one a rough idea of how those who should, and probably do, know better cave in under political pressures on nuclear issues.

The objections to crisis relocation were legion. The media, Congress, academia, and sundry others heaped scorn on a proposal that they said was incredible. How can one expect U.S. city dwellers, who have a genius for snarling up traffic in peacetime, to evacuate in any orderly fashion under the terror of impending nuclear war? Even without nuclear mushrooms looming near, how can one expect American city dwellers, as independent a breed as exists, to cooperate in peacetime evacuation exercises? What would be the reaction of those who did cooperate and left town when they returned to find that some of those who stayed had looted their homes and businesses? With these kinds of questions rampant around the country, the administration was forced to beat a retreat from its proposal for crisis-relocation civil defense.

If anything, the administration proposal turned out to be counterproductive, as has been the case in the past when similar proposals were made. The cause of civil defense suffered a severe setback and the matter was practically dropped from the nuclear debate. And the tragedy of it is, had the government told it as it is and explained to the American people that at least on the Soviet side there was no intention of wiping out the world, including the United States, a sensible civil defense system could have been proposed which could have gotten broad acceptance by the people. But this would have been telling the people that nuclear war was possible, which today is felt by politicians, including presidents, to carry the risk of political suicide. What good will it do to square off with the people by telling them the facts when your political opponent, careless of the facts when he smells a chance of beating you in the next election, will appeal to the people's emotions in an attempt to hurt your political image?*

As to what kind of civil defense would be most realistic, in the framework of the Soviet nuclear strategy discussed above, the answer is, clearly, the *stay-put* kind. This would involve the construction of very simple underground shelters in most urban areas, designed primarily to provide protection against the fallout radiation resulting from attacks against distant military targets and from the effects of nonnuclear, or extremely low-yield nuclear, attacks on nearby military production targets. (In many cases, existing underground construction could be modified to allow highly satisfactory shelters.) Neighborhood shelters could be occupied within a fraction of an hour so that protection could be achieved even in the event of a surprise attack, with essentially none of the horrendous problems associated with an evacuation plan.

---

* Many years ago an acquaintance of mine, who had been an adviser on nuclear-weapon issues to Adlai Stevenson in the 1956 presidential campaign, told me the following tale: Stevenson's key political advisers had convinced him that the only way of getting an effective campaign theme was to charge Eisenhower with dangerous recklessness in his determination to continue nuclear testing, even though it wasn't so, as my acquaintance tried to persuade Stevenson. Stevenson's response couldn't have been more candid, as he explained that the nuclear issue was his only hope; there was nothing else to bring up that could make Eisenhower look bad. Politics was politics.

What is not generally understood is that building underground shelters to protect against the fallout radiation (which can also protect against nonnuclear weapons) also provides substantial protection against blast. In fact, in most cases the blast resistance is far more than required, the reason being that Soviet strategy calls for nuclear warheads of vastly smaller explosive power than the Armageddon levels put forth by those who attempt to demonstrate that effective civil defense is impossible.

As to the cost of a simple stay-put shelter program for an urban area, since this approach has not been favored by the government, the government has not chosen to sponsor studies which would estimate such cost. However, based on an elementary consideration of requirements for such a system, a rough estimate is that it might cost some tens of billions of dollars, certainly well below $100 billion. An effective civil defense system designed to save millions and millions of lives would, it seems to me, be a far better investment than putting the money into offensive weapon systems such as the MX missile, whose effectiveness is disputed and doubtful. When President Reagan, in advancing his ABM proposal for defending our country against ballistic missile attack, declared that saving lives is morally preferable to avenging them (which would happen if we retaliated with MX missiles), why didn't he use this moral thesis sensibly to propose an urban civil defense program? Had he done so, chances are he could have not only gained the support of the American people, but also let himself off the hook on the MX, which did not have the people's support, and proceeded posthaste on the mobile Midgetman ICBM, which had most everyone's support.

The moral argument that Ronald Reagan made in 1983 for ABM in his historic "Star Wars" speech was at least as compelling as that made by Richard Nixon in 1969. So far, however, the Reagan administration's track record for doing something about ABM has been far from compelling. When the backlash from the U.S. anti-defense community hit the fan, the administration began to back away from any sense of urgency and priority. In setting up planning requirements for an ABM program, the Pentagon made clear that it was viewing the problem on a "long-range (to post-2000 era)" basis and was emphasizing "effectiveness rather than potential for early deployment." As a standard for evaluating advanced ABM technologies, impossibly high levels of efficiency, 99-plus percent, were called for; such, in effect, made sure that in the foreseeable future the American people would have no defense against ballistic missile attack.

Like that on the civil defense issue, the debate, on both sides of the fence, over Reagan's proposal was conducted within exactly the wrong framework; namely, that the Soviet nuclear strategy involved dispatching thousands of nuclear warheads against U.S. cities. Within this framework, those outside the government opposed to ABM were able to argue that even if 1 percent, or .01 percent, of the warheads were able to penetrate the defenses, the result would be a catastrophe beyond comprehension. Moreover, contended the opposition, the cost of any ABM system designed to achieve such fantastic efficiencies would be out of sight, maybe even a trillion dollars, or more. Maybe the opposition was right; but there is no conceivable way of finding out, short of having at least one nuclear war so that its claims can be checked.

As for those in the government, afraid to talk about such politically disastrous things as nuclear-war fighting and nuclear-war outcomes, which their boss, the president, had cast in a hopeless, losing context, they too cast the problem in the realm of unreality. They sought to preserve the ABM option the president had opted for, by stalling on a decision into the next century. This may have satisfied their boss, but it did nothing to help preserve nuclear deterrence over the years before the next century, years that will be dangerous without such defense.

In trying to analyze the ABM problem realistically, four fundamental observations must be made. First, to pursue an ABM program in the absence of a civil defense program is simply ludicrous. Second, to pursue an ABM program in the absence of pursuing defenses against other nuclear threats will not provide meaningful security over the long run. Third, to pursue an ABM program (or any other active defense program) on the basis of threat attrition rates approaching 100 percent practically ensures that the program will never come to fruition. Fourth, an ABM program must be planned on a time scale that is commensurate with the threat of nuclear war, and this does not involve planning for the next century—the threat is already seriously with us and must be dealt with as quickly as is practical.

Regarding the first observation, considering the horror of nuclear war, which has permeated so much of the American psyche, to expect that an unsheltered U.S. populace will not suffer a massive societal collapse has to be whistling Dixie. The nation, in all probability, would fall apart at the seams and the president (or his successor, who might be very far down the totem pole in view of the priority the Soviets give to neutralizing the U.S. political leadership in the event of war), lacking any real public support for carrying on a war, might have little choice except to sue for peace—on Russian terms. (The need to keep up the morale of the Soviet population during a nuclear war has been a primary impetus behind the Russians' civil defense program.)

Although the bulk of the Soviet strategic nuclear offensive capabilities appears to be in the form of ballistic missiles, other weapons, such as cruise missiles, have been developed for attack on the United States. Moreover, as we have discussed, the Soviet force of modern bombers probably already has intercontinental range and must be taken into account. These are threats against which an ABM system may be of precious little effectiveness. Which dictates a requirement for a complementary air-defense system, if our overall active defenses are to be of real worth.

If one examines the record of active defenses there is no foundation in past fact to allow any confidence whatsoever that a future ABM system can have a level of efficiency even remotely approaching 100 percent. There are simply too many degrading factors involved: the maintenance of extremely complicated equipment by less than perfect human beings; the reliability of this equipment in the unpredictable environment of nuclear war; and countermeasures the enemy may devise. All these factors can seriously reduce the theoretical efficiency of any system. The truth of the matter is, there is no way of predicting how efficient an ABM system may be when the moment of truth arrives.

What can be said, however, is that if we set our performance requirements too high we stand a sizable risk of getting far less performance than we require. We also stand the risk of paying far too much money to get it, maybe even as much money as ABM opponents have claimed, which will be far more money than the Congress is willing to provide.

For reasons discussed earlier, we cannot dismiss the possibility of nuclear war. To set up ABM requirements on the premise that this possibility will not be a serious one over the next decade or two is to ignore the realities of the world around us; in particular, the nuclear realities of the Soviet Union. As such, in planning for an ABM system, a first-generation capability should be based on the same approach we took on the atomic bomb in World War II; namely, the establishment of an ABM Manhattan Project holding the highest priority in the Defense Department.

104

The most practical and realistic approach toward establishing ABM requirements is to begin by casting the problem in the context of the Soviet nuclear threat and the strategy underlying the threat. Having done this, it then becomes possible to determine just what is to be defended against nuclear attack in the United States; and how, in turn, such defense can best help protect the American people, their lives and their freedom. And in taking this approach, it will be not only necessary to consider the most effective technology, but also necessary that this technology permits an ABM system having a cost that is acceptable to the Congress and the taxpayer. In all probability, this can be accomplished only by a system exploiting nuclear-warhead technology.

Appearing on "Meet the Press" in 1983, Defense Secretary Caspar Weinberger, discussing the president's "Star Wars" ABM proposal, stressed the necessity "to get a basically thoroughly reliable defense against incoming missiles, the opportunity to destroy the missiles preferably by nonnuclear means in—in—outside the atmosphere. And once this is achieved, and I'm confident it can be achieved, then you would have a new means of keeping the strategic balance, which depended not on any kind of fear or any kind of retaliation, but on a proven ability to defend. And that is what I think would be the most satisfactory result we can have, given the state of today's world." The secretary's objective, echoing that expressed by the president, couldn't have been nobler. But his preferred means, "nonnuclear" means, for achieving it couldn't have been more unrealistically related to the realities of the Soviet threat to the United States, which happens to be a *nuclear* threat.

On what conceivable grounds would a nonnuclear ABM system be preferable to a nuclear system, when thousands of nuclear warheads are threatening the very existence of the United States? Why is it preferable to have a system that must be "thoroughly reliable," which can destroy incoming missiles "outside the atmosphere," when the odds are that such a system will have such stringent design requirements as to make it least reliable, most expensive (maybe unacceptably expensive), most vulnerable to enemy countermeasures, and least available in time, where time is of so great an essence?

As to the first question, if the objective of an ABM system is to be able to thwart Soviet plans for nuclear attack on the United States to a degree that such attack can be deterred, nothing should deter us from seeking the most effective system that technology can provide. This technology has to be nuclear for reasons that ought to be obvious to anyone, the same reasons why offensive strategic weapons always have incorporated nuclear warheads. Practically any nuclear device, that can pack such a fantastic amount of energy in so small a package, is bound to provide a far more effective, reliable, and cheaper ABM system than one based on a nonnuclear (that is, chemical) energy source.

Behind Weinberger's nonnuclear preference are political considerations having to do with the longstanding resistance to *nuclear* defensive weapons and a United States treaty signed many years ago that ostensibly banned nuclear weapons from space.

The antinuclear resistance in the United States stemmed mainly from the antinuclear community, which believed, incredible as this may sound, that relying on defensive nuclear warheads would put the U.S. in the immoral position of being the first to use nuclear weapons. How, in any compelling way, these arguments could be used with political effectiveness, when a lack of defenses could result in the demise of our country, would seem beyond rational comprehension; but this indeed has been very much the case.

As for the U.N. treaty, if one examines the language, we note that the weapons to be banned from space are those of "mass destruction." What this clearly implies is that they are offensive weapons that can be launched from space to cause massive destruction on earth. To apply this ban to defensive nuclear warheads that might be used in space-based systems is ridiculous, for two reasons: (1) their very design would make it infeasible to use them in an offensive mode against targets on earth; and (2) the warhead technologies involved do not call for explosive powers required in offensive nuclear weapons that could provide "mass destruction" as it is defined in the U.N. treaty, which stems from the devastation inflicted by the bombings of Hiroshima and Nagasaki. So what we see here, even in those in government who say they support the president's "Star Wars" proposal, is a political subservience to arms-control treaties that even seem to hint at banning nuclear warheads in space, but whose specific terms do not foreclose on defensive applications of these warheads.

As to the second question, you will recall that the major thrust of the "Star Wars" proposal was toward the establishment of a space-based system, consisting of a number of satellites that could detect, track, and then destroy ballistic missiles within the first few minutes after launch. This would be during the so-called boost phase of flight, when the enormous amount of heat generated by the rocket engines supposedly would make the missile an easy target to find and destroy by such exotic kill mechanisms as laser beams and swarms of small heat-seeking rockets traveling at extremely high speed.

The supposedly great advantage of that defensive scheme is its ability to destroy the enemy missiles before their individual warheads are released. Depending upon the particular Russian missile being attacked, a kill during the boost phase will prevent as many as ten or twenty, or even more for the largest missiles, nuclear explosions from taking place on targets in the United States. Surely sounds far better than a scheme dependent on waiting until tens of thousands of nuclear warheads come within range of an ABM system based on U.S. terra firma. Or does it?

Underlying this great advantage claimed for the "Star Wars" approach is the fallacious implication that the Soviet nuclear threat will not be very much different in the next century from what it is now. What seems to have been assumed is that if we seriously took this approach, the Soviets would not seriously begin to take measures to redesign their missile capabilities so that by the time a "Star Wars" system materialized, they could neutralize its effectiveness. In many ways this issue is quite similar to that of the claims being made for U.S. advanced conventional weapons, where we would be able to detect and destroy the Red Army's second-echelon armored forces long before they reached the front lines and were capable of destroying our forces. In this respect there are any number of ways the Soviets, using nuclear means, could devise (having plenty of time to do so) methods for killing our satellites (maybe even using "Star Wars" technology) or take countermeasures (such as heat decoys) against our missile kill mechanisms. Or they might elect to diversify their arsenal of offensive nuclear weapons (again, having plenty of time to do so) to include supersonic cruise missiles (launched from submarines and the USSR), bombers (which they are producing), and perhaps even satellite bombardment systems (which they began to explore many years ago)—none of those systems being vulnerable to a "Star Wars" defensive system.

For these kinds of reasons, we should give serious thought to revising our approach to defending our country against nuclear attack and consider taking a two-track approach: both with the highest national priority.

The "Star Wars" program should be accelerated to a much higher level of effort than currently exists so that we can determine, as soon as possible, the potential of this approach. We should do so, however, without shackling technology so that all approaches, especially nuclear approaches, can be assessed. Giving technology a free rein can produce miracles in short order. In this respect, I would remind you of the U.S. ICBM program which about thirty years ago President Dwight Eisenhower established at top national priority.

When the ICBM program was being formulated there were doubting Thomases galore, in the military and scientific ranks, who maintained that the missile would never fly. I remember visiting the headquarters of the U.S. Strategic Air Command in 1953, at which time I had an audience with the commander, Gen. Curtis LeMay, who told me that he didn't expect to see the missile operational in his lifetime. Five years later it was operational; LeMay was still alive and kicking. Nuclear-weapon experts predicted that it would not be possible to develop a lightweight megaton thermonuclear warhead for the missile within the scheduled development time. This was accomplished well within this time. A member of the ICBM steering committee who was an expert on guidance told me that it would be a miracle if the missile were able to hit within five miles of the target. It turned out to be more like one mile. Doubts were expressed that reentry vehicle materials could be developed to keep the vehicle from burning up when it came back into the atmosphere. The doubts turned out to be unfounded. And so on.

Whereas nobody can predict the outcome of a "Star Wars" program carried on with the same zeal and dedication of the ICBM project, based on this extremely successful precedent there is no reason to be unduly pessimistic. However, I say this on the premise that the program will be conducted on a realistic basis that does not include a requirement for impossibly high levels of effectiveness. Rather, the program should be based on a realistic appraisal of the Soviet nuclear strategy—which is to attack a huge number of military targets all over the U.S. to bring about our capitulation, but not U.S. cities—for efficiency levels well below 100 percent can be very effective in thwarting the Soviet strategy. If this tack is taken, it may be possible to develop space-based defensive systems that can effectively cope with countermeasures the Soviets can be expected to develop, for it will become practical to apply a greater amount of effort to this objective. And in the meantime, we should come down to earth and proceed with an ABM system, which in large measure can exploit already developed technologies not encumbered with "Star Wars" countermeasures problems, and which can be available far sooner than any "Star Wars" system.

For many years the U.S. Army has been doing research and development on ABM systems based on using low-yield nuclear warheads in surface-to-air missiles to destroy incoming enemy warheads. Despite the considerable progress that has been made, it has not come to a point where these systems can cope economically with the threat from Soviet multiple-warhead missiles. For such systems to be cost-effective, new technologies must be applied that presently do not appear in sight.

Perhaps the major reason why the approach taken thus far has failed to yield cost-effective results is that it has been too conventional in nature. Although it has been based on using nuclear explosives, there has been relatively little attention paid to how nuclear explosives might be applied to produce a warhead kill mechanism making it possible to do away with the defensive missile. In other words, might it be possible to have a low-yield nuclear explosive of a design very different from current versions, which device, positioned at the surface, could project an extremely high velocity beam of enemy warhead-killing effects at a considerable distance above the military installation to be protected, and be able to destroy the warhead before it detonated? By taking this tack, we would, at least in principle, be working in the direction of a much simpler and cheaper system, offering the possibility for a truly cost-effective ABM defense.

The surface-to-air ABM missiles under development and exploration over the years have had a number of intrinsic drawbacks, making them cost-ineffective. The missiles themselves, to destroy the incoming warheads, traveling at enormous speed, in time, have to be of very high performance. This calls for a minimum-size and -weight missile requiring a highly sophisticated microminiaturized technology, which works to drive up the missile cost. Moreover, it calls for a minimum-size nuclear warhead, which in turn drives up the warhead cost; very small nuclear warheads can be very costly, being more complicated in design and having to use more expensive fissile material than larger versions. Finally, when a number of nuclear-armed defensive missiles have to be fired at numerous incoming offensive warheads, there are serious problems regarding fratricidal effects (the detonation of one missile warhead destroying another missile launched in its vicinity) and defensive warhead bursts degrading the tracking radar's ability to see the incoming enemy warheads (known as radar blackout).

On the other hand, for a ground-based nuclear system none of these drawbacks need exist. Since the performance requirement is easily met by the high-velocity beam (which for certain applications can travel close to the speed of light), the defensive weapon itself need have no significant size and weight constraints. As such there is no requirement for highly expensive high-technology components, which can drive up missile costs excessively. Moreover, since there is no serious constraint on the size and weight of the nuclear warhead, which does not have to go anywhere at very high speed, it can be of simpler design, use less fissile material, and thus be substantially cheaper than a missile warhead. Finally, being ground-based, the explosive effects of such a system readily can be shielded to a degree where no fratricidal or radar blackout problems exist. (If you're wondering about the effects of these low-yield explosions on the personnel and facilities of the military installations to be defended, it goes without saying that if these targets are important enough to be attacked, they will be hardened anyway against the effects of far higher-yield offensive nuclear explosions, as we long have been doing with our ICBMs. So the problem, in effect, will have solved itself.)

As to the nature of such defensive nuclear weapons, which are known as directed-effects weapons, a number of schemes may be feasible.

Perhaps the simplest and most straightforward approach would be to use the nuclear explosive to accelerate an enormous number of small projectiles to hypervelocity speeds. This could be called a nuclear shotgun, so to speak. There being no serious weight constraints on such a device, the number of projectiles required to ensure destruction of enemy warheads could be practically guaranteed.

During the late 1970s an impressive amount of evidence was reported which strongly indicated that the Soviets had set to work on a particle beam ABM defensive system based on low-yield nuclear explosions. This entailed utilizing the energy from these explosions to accelerate subatomic particles to velocities approaching the speed of light. However, because the Soviets were not so obliging as to invite us in to see what was going on, there was no way to make a factual determination of exactly what they were up to. Theoretical analysis, based on what little we could glean from our satellite reconnaissance, did not dispute the possibility that such

110

a system was feasible, holding a "Star Wars" potential on earth, where the energy from one nuclear explosive could be harnessed to destroy a number of incoming warheads. And had such a project actually been under way in the USSR, nothing similar was going on in the U.S. There should have been.

The two ABM concepts discussed above hardly represent anything dramatically new. Scientists in our nuclear weapon laboratories have been aware of such possibilities for many years. The main obstacle in the way of intensively researching these possibilities, plus others based on nuclear explosives, has been, of course, politics. So great has been the political resistance to defensive schemes using nuclear explosives, that it has been impossible to assign priority requirements for exploring such concepts, despite the promise they offer—a far greater promise than any nonnuclear schemes. Had such requirements been assigned to the laboratories, the challenge gladly would have been picked up by the more imaginative scientists who were chafing over how pedestrian their work had become.

The antinuclear politics against nuclear defense has become so intense as to be blinded to the realities of the issue. The realities are very simple.

If there is no effective defense of our military installations, we are risking the possibility that the Soviets may one day decide to attack them, to win quickly a nuclear war because our military capabilities would have been quickly destroyed. Moreover, such an attack will not only cost us our freedom, but also produce severe postwar recovery problems, even if we had an effective civil defense system. An effective civil defense may indeed save the lives of most Americans. But without an effective active defense against nuclear attack, the damage to the rural fabric, where most nuclear targets are located, will very likely be enormous. Large areas of farmlands will be burned and heavily contaminated with radioactivity. And the cities will probably be contaminated to a degree where those in civil defense shelters will have to wait much longer before they can emerge to the surface. Most important, however, without an effective defense, we are risking the credibility of our deterrent policy, a risk that we simply cannot afford to take.

So when our government defers to the perceived antinuclear political realities and states a preference for defending our country by nonnuclear means, stating that this "would be the most satisfactory result we can have, given the state of today's world," I can only note that our government's assessment of the state of today's world has to be entirely unsatisfactory—and dangerous. A U.S. government acting truly in the interests of the American people should address itself to the realities of today's world in deciding on how to defend our country, and not be dictated to by political mythologies.

If we did decide to protect ourselves against nuclear attack, with both passive and active measures, how much would it cost? Although the American people always have said, when polled on the subject, that they would be willing to pay the price for an effective defense, they were hardly implying that they would accept anything that began to push taxes out of sight. We are already seeing this in the form of widespread resistance to the increased military budget proposed by the Reagan administration. Defense at any price, when cast in economic reality, really means that the price has to be right.

Practically every U.S. administration since the end of World War II has maintained that to have a healthy national defense establishment, we first need to have a healthy economy. Whereas this requirement does not necessarily reflect either military or economic logic, it surely does reflect U.S. political logic; that's the way it is.

In this respect, if the government did decide on a full-scale crash program for civil defense and active defense, and the estimated cost turned out to be huge (say, hundreds of billions of dollars over the next several years); were it proposed that this cost be tacked onto the existing military budget, it could be confidently predicted that this would be rejected out of hand by the American taxpayer. Even were it to offer the best prospect of avoiding nuclear war, the prospect of a much greater budget deficit, or greater taxes, or both, and the greater threat to our economic health would in all probability succeed in killing the proposal. Not that this would be a logical reaction; it's just that, that's the way it is.

On the other hand, let's assume that the taxpayer finally realizes that the greatest threat of nuclear war—a considerable threat to his pocketbook as well—comes from our policy of intervening in foreign wars to defend other countries, and that this policy consumes most of our military budget, which is now about $300 billion a year. Should he revolt against this dangerous policy and its excessively high budget, odds are that there would be more than enough money available to foot the bill for the defense and survival of our own country.

How much more money might be available, I really don't know.

112

Nor does anybody else. That would depend on the pricetag for passive (civil) and active defense, particularly the latter.

Civil defense is a quantity amenable to reasonable calculation, since the parameters involved are reasonably understood. Such a calculation is based on the number of neighborhood shelters needed to give fallout protection to the U.S. population. Since we long have known the costs of such shelters, the price of civil defense readily can be determined. As I mentioned before, it probably will cost on the order of some tens of billions of dollars. That cost might sound huge, but is small potatoes compared with the cost of our conventional forces.

As for the cost of an effective active defense system, since we have yet to undertake such, the pricetag is now largely an unknown quantity. What can be said, however, is that it will not be anywhere near the cost of fielding and maintaining our conventional forces to implement our overseas intervention policy. And whatever it may be, chances are the taxpayer will gladly pay the price for his protection and survival.

I would like to believe, with full intellectual vanity, that the arguments made here on the necessity to achieve a defense against nuclear attack will be found persuasive by the reader. But I've been around too long to know that this isn't likely to happen. If one were to survey the history of our major new weapon developments and what has sired them, he would discover that more likely than not they have come about because of what the Russians have done.

The principal reason we embarked on our ICBM program was that our intelligence had determined that the Soviets already had done so. Even then, when a Soviet ICBM capability failed to materialize, our ICBM production program began to slacken—until Sputnik went into orbit in 1957, whereupon Washington went into a state of panic and our program went into high gear. Such trauma also produced our first determined effort to get cracking on ABM. A new agency was created in the Pentagon, charged with the technological exploration of advanced ABM concepts, including space-based systems similar in nature to some of the "Star Wars" concepts. But nothing of real consequence happened.

In the mid-1960s, when we saw definite signs of a Soviet ABM development, we again began getting serious about ABM. But when nothing of moment seemed to be happening in the Soviet Union, we became less serious, until the late 1960s, when the significance of the tremendous Soviet ICBM buildup was realized and an alarmed President Nixon made a dramatic appeal for support for his Safeguard ABM program. Which he proceeded to sell out in the SALT I treaty, while he reversed himself in the new spirit of détente, and backed away from his earlier tocsin sounding. With the signing of the SALT I treaty, our ABM program went into low gear, a situation which has continued to the present, with no real expectation that a U.S. ABM capability will materialize during this century. That is, unless the Russians once again do something to shake us: like, for example, breaking off from the ABM treaty (which they've already violated in numerous ways) and breaking out with a full-fledged nationwide ABM capability. And there are increasing signs that they may be on the verge of doing exactly that.

Should that happen, I daresay although such has long been predicted, for very good reasons, we would go into a terrible state of shock. Our fervent, almost desperate, hopes that nuclear war can be avoided via nuclear arms control would have been shattered. Worse yet, however, would be the great insecurity that would descend upon us, with the realization that our hopes for avoiding nuclear war through our strategy of deterrence would have been dealt a crippling blow. In no small way has our deterrent strategy been cast in the framework of the ABM treaty. With the sudden emergence of a Soviet ABM capability, this strategy, involving our ability to retaliate effectively against the USSR after being attacked, would be cast into serious doubt. Suddenly we would be facing extremely insecure years ahead, not knowing how effective the Soviet ABM system might be, but fearful that it might be highly effective.

With this state of shock, I think it is safe to say that all of a sudden whatever misgivings the government might have had over ABM would suddenly disappear, and with a tremendous sense of urgency it would begin to move. In what direction it might move to acquire an ABM capability as quickly as possible, the government as of now, I suspect, hasn't the wildest idea. In all probability, it would be caught with its pants down, as happened when Sputnik suddenly appeared in the skies. Which strongly suggests that the government should start preparing a contingency program right now, so that it could at least get started in an orderly and sensible way.

In his "Star Wars" speech, Ronald Reagan hoped that American scientists could bring about the day when a defense against offensive nuclear missiles could relegate those missiles to the junkyard:

"I call upon the scientific community in our country, those who gave us nuclear weapons, to turn their great talents now to the cause of mankind and world peace: to give us the means of rendering these nuclear weapons impotent and obsolete." The president's vision may have been lofty, but I'm afraid he set his sights too high. The day probably will never arrive. In the meantime, however, besides trying to work toward a sensible defense against Russian nuclear missiles, we should be trying to make some sense out of our own missiles, especially the ICBMs.

One of the sorriest episodes in our nuclear-weapon history was that of the MX. At the beginning of its development, two requirements received the greatest emphasis.

First, it was becoming clear during the late 1970s that Soviet ICBM accuracies were improving to a point where our Minuteman ICBMs (a thousand of them in hardened silos) were becoming extremely vulnerable to a Soviet nuclear first strike. Since Minuteman was judged to be the most important weapon in our strategic arsenal, but was getting pretty old (having been developed during the late 1950s), it was deemed imperative that we get cracking on a new missile whose basing mode would allow it to survive nuclear attack. It would have to survive not only a first strike, but subsequent attacks as well in an extended nuclear war, on which the new PD-59 strategy was based. In an effort to meet this requirement—survivability—most experts agreed that the new missiles must have some degree of mobility so that the Russians would not be able at any time to target them for destruction.

Second, in view of the new PD-59 strategy, which required a capability to knock out heavily protected targets in the USSR (missiles in silos, military command posts, political leadership centers, etc.), the new missile would have to be pretty big. A big missile was needed to be able to deliver a large number of high-yield warheads with great accuracy against this complex of heavily hardened Russian targets. At least that's what the missile designers asserted was necessary.

Primarily based on these two specifications, the MX program was cranked up and went into high gear. Whereupon we discovered something that we should have known all along; namely, that big missiles and missile mobility are not very compatible. The Carter administration found this out when it proposed the so-called Race Track system, which had the missiles moving around, in enormous trailers, over thousands and thousands of acres, from one hardened shelter to another. Not only did this scheme send the cost of the system spiraling; it also got the environmentalists up in arms. And it still failed to appease many critics in Congress and the media who weren't satisfied as to its vulnerability to nuclear attack.

One sharp critic of the Race Track system was Ronald Reagan, whose presidential campaign in 1980 heavily emphasized the "window of vulnerability" of our ICBM forces, with a commitment to produce a truly survivable MX, which he said was essential to our security. However, when his administration tried to live up to his commitment, it bumped into the same facts of life as had its predecessors—there was no acceptable way to get a mobile MX system. In desperation, the Pentagon, citing a fantastic break-through in super-hardened silo technology, proposed the noto-rious Dense Pack concept, which the equally desperate White House accepted. But very few others did (even the Joints Chiefs of Staff split on the matter) and Dense Pack reached an ignominious end.

President Reagan, however, for political reasons, was hell-bent on getting approval for MX from the Congress. To achieve this end, he established the famous bipartisan Scowcroft Commission to bail him out. Which it did by declaring away the "window of vulnerability," maintaining that it never really did exist, even though several commission members previously had accepted, and worried about, its existence. Having shut the window, the com-mission cleared the way to base 100 MXs in silos, where most everyone agreed they would be sitting ducks for Soviet nuclear attack and thereby be unavailable to implement the PD-59 strategy they were conceived to implement. Also, as part of the overall package, the commission, to appease those in Congress who still worried about our ICBM vulnerability and those who were con-cerned over the arms-control aspects of MX, recommended a long-term development of the small mobile, single-warhead Midgetman ICBM. A great triumph for the Washington political system, but a dismal performance by Washington toward increasing the na-tion's security, which will become only increasingly insecure—for all the perfectly valid reasons that candidate Reagan warned about in 1980.

As of this writing, the fate of MX is highly uncertain. It may not survive, and even if it does, there is no way that it can contribute meaningfully to our security. At the same time, the ground rules determining the nature of the Midgetman design have been so unrealistically fashioned as virtually to ensure its rejection when, sometime in the 1990s, its development is completed and a deployment plan proposed to the Congress.

For reasons having to do with domestic politics and nuclear arms control, Midgetman deployment would be confined to government military reservations.

The political reason arises from the almost certain public outcry that would result if attempts were made to deploy it uninhibitedly around the country. Most people are queasy over the idea of nuclear-armed missiles, ready to be fired, roaming through their neighborhoods. Moreover, in an era of increasing terrorism, there would be the fear of terrorist attack, including the possibility that the nuclear warhead might be captured.

The arms-control constraint arises from the concern that a nuclear-weapon system spread all over the country would pose serious verification problems were this system to be governed by an arms-control treaty. In fact, by its very nature, a countrywide small mobile missile system should be deployed in a manner that would make observation by an enemy most difficult, and thus most enhance its survivability. In the current arms-control climate, unrealistic as it may be, there would be screaming from the rooftops over such deployment. Which is why Midgetman now is planned for deployment on government reservations, where it will be easy for Soviet spy satellites to keep tabs on the number of missiles, to make sure the treaty limits are being observed.

The fundamental drawback of a Midgetman system deployed on a military reservation is that there simply isn't enough room to guarantee its survival over the long run. By the long run, we're talking about a deployment period well into the next century, which would give the Russians all the time in the world to devise means for finding and destroying missiles confined to such a limited area. It would also give Midgetman opponents in the U.S. all the time in the world to devise such means for the Russians to take, as MX opponents have been busily doing over the years. In all probability, long before Midgetman is ready for production, these U.S. opponents, whose ranks include some of the brightest scientists in the country, will have figured out enough schemes to defeat the missile to be able to convince the Congress and the media that the missile shouldn't be built.

There is another drawback of Midgetman, as presently under design, which probably will lend fuel to opposition fires, a drawback that need not be. The missile is being designed to fulfill the MX targeting role; that is, to have a capability to knock out heavily

117

hardened Soviet targets in accordance with the dictates of PD-59. Such a requirement will succeed only in increasing the size and complexity of the missile to a degree where its high cost may imperil its acceptance, completely apart from objections over its basing mode.

For reasons brought out earlier, having to do with Soviet concealment and the high probability that seemingly hard targets are actually decoys to force a wasteful expenditure of our weapons, there would seem to be no compelling need to have a hard-target kill capability. The missile should be designed for use against classes of targets that cannot be easily concealed and decoyed; and doing this will allow a substantial reduction in system cost. Admittedly, this might not be the most effective way to fight a war, but I'm afraid there is precious little that we can do about it. On the other hand, if we go about designing our own nuclear forces properly, we can effectively offset this targeting imbalance. That can be accomplished by developing and deploying a force of mobile missiles that can operate during peacetime over the full extent of the land, unobservable and thus unattackable by the Soviets.

Right after World War II, Los Alamos and the U.S. Air Force, which then had custody of all the atomic bombs, worked out an ingenious warhead design which allowed the fissile material to be kept separate from the rest of the bomb. Only when the bomber approached target would the material be inserted into the bomb. Incorporating such a design into our stockpile would have eliminated concerns over the possibility of a low-order nuclear explosion resulting from accidental detonation of the bomb's high explosive assembly. It also would have greatly reduced the possibility of such a detonation causing the widespread dispersal of highly toxic fissile material.

The design, however, had one serious drawback: it called for much more fissile material than one not having an insertable feature. Since that was in an era where fissile material was in very short supply and, for good reasons, the United States wanted to have the largest stockpile of bombs possible, the idea, despite its basic attractiveness, was not picked up. But that was close to forty years ago, when our nuclear-warhead technology was in its infancy.

Today, a drastically different situation exists. Not only can we produce nuclear warheads having this insertable feature, called Insertable Nuclear Capsule (INC) warheads, which are highly efficient in their use of fissile material, but this material is running out our ears. There is no good reason not to take advantage of INC technology where it can be of advantage, and one place where it can be of great advantage is in a Midgetman missile designed to provide a truly survivable deployment mode. The mode would involve spreading the weapon system around the entirety of the country and in peacetime disassembling it into three parts: a rocket booster; a reentry vehicle (RV) containing an INC nuclear warhead and the missile guidance and control equipment; and the INC.

The rocket boosters, which would constitute the great bulk of the missile's size and weight (perhaps thirty feet in length and weighing about twenty thousand pounds), would be carried in standard commercial tractor-semis, indistinguishable on the outside from those found by the thousands on U.S. highways and country roads. The boosters would use a solid propellant, a fuel very difficult to ignite by sabotage and extremely difficult by accident. Even were the propellant to be ignited, the danger to the immediate surroundings would be less than that from a regular gasoline truck catching fire. However, the actual danger would be even much less, since the semis would be instructed to stay away from populated areas, spending most of their time in rural areas. In this mobile deployment mode, the booster system would blend into the normal commercial transportation environment and be essentially unobservable by Soviet reconnaissance satellites.

The reentry vehicles (a few feet in length and weighing maybe a couple of hundred pounds) would be stored in small, cheap, short takeoff and landing (STOL) transport aircraft of the kinds seen today by the thousands operating out of hundreds of airports around the U.S. Flying out of secure military bases around the country, these aircraft, carrying maybe one or two handfuls of RVs, would spend most of their time aloft. Every several hours they would return to base for a crew change and refueling. The flight pattern for the STOLs would be designed so that at any time, day or night, most of the aircraft would blend into the commercial pattern. Having the ability to take off and land in only several hundred feet of surface (including soft fields, if necessary), they could rendezvous with the booster trucks at practically any point of arrangement. At a given rendezvous, a RV would be removed from the airplane and quickly attached to the booster. The procedure would be simple and straightforward, one that has been used for many years in our tactical nuclear missiles.

Similarly, the INCs also would be stored in the STOLs operating

119

from secure military bases, where each STOL would carry maybe one or two handfuls of INCs. To prevent the possibility of radioactive contamination in case of a crash, the INCs would be kept in crashproof containers. The containers, which already have been designed, would have a special "lock and key" security system known only to the aircraft crew, thereby making it extremely difficult for unauthorized persons to get access to the contents. Still another feature of the containers is a mechanism for rendering the fissile material useless in making a nuclear explosive—just in case someone did get his hands on a container and try to force it open and make off with the nuclear capsule. Upon rendezvous with the booster trucks and the RVs, the capsules could readily be inserted into the nuclear warheads. The missile would now be ready for launching.

Having described the general nature of such an ICBM, let's now take stock of its key advantages.

First and foremost, this missile concept would offer the most realistic opportunity to close the window of vulnerability. With such a system in place, a serious threat of a Soviet first strike would no longer exist. This would hold true even if the Soviets were one day to achieve a capability to find and destroy our nuclear missile submarines, which in the future will consist of smaller numbers of giant-size Trident subs; or to catch our bombers on their bases and destroy them with nuclear weapons before they could get safely away. In other words, by taking away from the Soviets the ability to target our ICBMs, we can equalize the targeting gap that most likely exists because of Soviet deception and disinformation practices. We can't destroy their missiles; they can't destroy our missiles; which ought to make us supremely happy, for in no small way would such a state of affairs enhance deterrence.

Next, such a system should pretty much dispel the concerns of those who worry, with some justification, about the unauthorized use of our strategic nuclear weapons or the possibility that a trigger-happy president might be willing to launch his vulnerable ICBMs after receiving "unequivocal" notification from his early-warning network that a Soviet first nuclear strike is under way.

By its nature, this system makes extremely remote the chances that some conspiratorial group could get together to plan an unauthorized missile launch one day. Besides having received the careful psychological screening that all personnel associated with nuclear weapons must go through, the tractor-semi and aircraft crews would have no reason to know each other—and thus no reason for a megalomaniacal collusion to gain "fame" as the chaps who started history's first nuclear war. We're not talking here about missile crews in silos or submarines, crews that practically live with each other. Instead, we are here speaking of people who would have no reason even to know each other; would normally be separated from each other by large distances; and would not even know where most of the others were—being told so only once the war was under way or suspected to be under way. Such would not be optimum circumstances in which to create a conspiracy, even were there a desire to conspire—which in itself is extremely improbable, and thus far has never been detected, even though the circumstances have been vastly more accommodating.

As for the worry over launch-on-warning, that simply isn't in the cards for this system. Long before the word could be got off to the different crews, the missile put together, and the firing button pushed, the Soviet warheads would have exploded. So forget about that worry; it isn't credible for such a system.

As noted, it makes little sense to give the Midgetman missile the capability of knocking out heavily hardened targets when these targets may not contain the things we want to destroy—like missiles and critical personnel. As mentioned, however, Midgetman is being designed to have this capability. But if we ever decided to scratch the Midgetman concept for a more realistic, truly mobile system, this capability should not be required. The requirement for a hard-target kill capability calls for a combination of a large-yield warhead and high delivery accuracy, both items coming at a price. Generally, the larger the yield the larger and heavier the warhead has to be, which in turn calls for a larger and heavier, and more costly, missile to deliver the warhead. Also, the achievement of high delivery accuracy calls for a highly refined guidance system and this does not come on the cheap. So were we ever to embark on a mobile ICBM program along more sensible lines than we're now doing, we might want to tailor its targeting requirements to the realities of the target system the Soviets might present us with. In which case we could do so at a significant reduction in the program's cost.

Finally, assuming that we did everything else needed to put some sense into the PD-59 targeting strategy (that is, providing civil defense, active defense, survivable command and control of our nuclear weapons, etc.), having an ICBM that could survive well into a nuclear war would at least give us the opportunity to look for targets we hadn't seen previously. And if we found them, to be able to attack them. Or to be able to reattack targets that we had missed on first attempt. In other words, it would give us the opportunity to carry on a war. Not that this is an appealing thought, but since it is the way the Russians view the matter, we would have the best deterrent posture by having this capability.

Were we ever to embark upon an ICBM program of the type just discussed, how many missiles should we build? Darned if I know, and I can assure you that nobody else is in a position to know; the reason is that we have no way of determining what kinds of targets and how many of them may be known to us when such a program is completed. As explained earlier, there is no reason to believe that the Soviets would want to be so obliging as to reveal their most important military goodies to us. There is every logical reason to believe that they would conceal these targets from our reconnaissance, and they have millions of square miles in which to do this. So how many missiles do we produce when there is no reliable way to determine how many we should produce?

Well, I would say that since there is no definitive answer to this question, we produce these missiles at a level the political traffic will bear. This has always been the case anyway. If the reader has any notions that the Defense Department ever has the ability to put out logically based weapon procurement requirements and that the Congress has logically acted on those requirements, for gosh sake, forget it. Even when we thought we knew what the enemy's strength was, there still were so many other uncertainties and intangibles as to make it virtually impossible to establish genuinely defensible requirements. This always has been basically a political process. But it is the way America operates its defense business. Except that in the nuclear age that's a pretty dangerous way to run a business—that is, business as usual.

However, for the same reason I would urge the highest priority for achieving an ABM capability, I would urge that we attach the same priority to a new survivable ICBM that Eisenhower did to our first ICBM program thirty years ago. Having a vulnerable ICBM system, as we now do, hardly serves to enhance deterrence. And since such a system would have essentially none of the technical obstacles to overcome that existed years ago, we could, if we really wanted to, have it in place well before this decade is out. That, however, would call for a sense of urgency that a few years ago was a hot presidential campaign political issue but today has been chilled by the political process. Still business as usual.

Yes, we can prevent nuclear war and *The Day After*:

● *If* our government changes our foreign policy back to what it was when our country came into being and determines not to intervene in foreign wars that are not of our making and really none of our business. It is surely in our interest that the rest of the world be at peace and be prosperous; but it is not in our vital interest to attempt to make this happen by deploying military forces around the world. As our history of military intervention since World War II has shown, it is decidedly against our vital interest when we make such attempts. And when we run the risk of nuclear war by such intervention, we are risking our supreme vital interest: survival. No foreign policy that holds this risk has the nation's real interest at heart. Our foreign policy does hold this risk. Our foreign policy must be changed to eliminate this risk, for it is intolerable, and thereby work toward avoiding nuclear war rather than producing it.

● *If* our government does what it is charged by the Constitution to do: provide for the "common defense" of the American people. A nation that cannot defend itself against nuclear attack hardly is in the best position to avoid nuclear attack, especially if the would-be attacker has taken means to defend itself. A nation in such a defenseless position is unduly risking its supreme vital interest: survival. Our current defense policy, by its own perverse nature, holds that having no protection against nuclear attack is the best way to avoid nuclear attack. This policy must be changed and the highest priorities be given to providing such protection.

● *If*—the most important *if* of all—Americans come to their senses and demand that their government make these changes. Unless the people come to understand that their government—by refusing to accept the realities of the nuclear age; being dominated by a foreign policy establishment living in the past; and succumbing to the politics of an enormous military-industrial complex seeking to expand its size and power (and profits)—is not acting in their best interest, that government, which really doesn't want to change its ways, will not change its ways. Only if the American people, who have much common sense, demand that their government take common-sense measures to avoid nuclear war, can we avoid nuclear war.

6

Can We Face the Issue?

A COUPLE OF YEARS AGO, I went off to a conference on world affairs where, naturally, nuclear war was the number one item on the agenda. One day during the conference I found myself in an impassioned argument with a learned Harvard professor (of psychology) on whether we could survive a nuclear war.

I took the position that I've taken in this book, that nuclear war wouldn't necessarily mean the end of everything. If we took the proper measures to survive, we could. And I made the stupid mistake of basing my claims on my longstanding professional expertise in this area. For my set of self-assumed good reasons, I let on that I was right and he was wrong.

He took the position that we couldn't survive, even if we did everything that I've recommended here, because we simply couldn't stand the societal (or psychological) trauma of nuclear war. Now he did so on the basis of many of the misperceptions of nuclear war that I've tried to correct here; and I tried to set him straight on his errors. Which was really stupid, because he really wasn't arguing as an expert on nuclear-war strategy and nuclear-weapons effects. Rather, his arguments traced to a conviction (undoubtedly stemming from his longstanding professional expertise) that American society was not psychologically equipped to withstand the horror of nuclear war. Completely apart from whatever the physical aspects of survival might be, the psychological aspects would do us in as a viable society.

Suddenly I realized that our argument was getting us no place in a hurry and I decided to divert the discussion down another path. Allowing that he might be right, although I wouldn't concede it, I declared that the really important issue was the avoidance of nuclear war; and here we certainly had no disagreement. Then I proceeded to explain our national policy of foreign military intervention with conventional forces and how this was enhancing the probability of nuclear war. Although he had had ample opportunity to find this out for himself, he hadn't; probably because nonnuclear weapons were involved and conventional war was something we could survive, especially if it were fought in somebody else's backyard.

Finally, after all that needless arguing, we were on common ground. He now realized that our policy for deterring nuclear war was being undercut by our conventional-war strategy. Having achieved this unity, I wasn't about to reintroduce my pitch for defense against nuclear attack. We parted company on the best of terms. However, on the issue of surviving nuclear war if deterrence were to fail, we were poles apart. I suspect we always will be. But I'm not convinced that I'm right and he's wrong.

Now I haven't the wildest idea how one goes about objectively appraising our societal vulnerability to nuclear war. I never thought to ask the Harvard professor how he pursued this matter; and had I asked him, for a number of reasons I would have found his explanation unacceptable. But not necessarily wrong.

On what nuclear-war scenario does one reach conclusions on societal survival? Since it is not possible to predict how a nuclear war might go, whatever scenario the professor may have adopted was bound to be in error. And thus his conclusions were bound to be in error; how much in error, heaven only knows. But that doesn't mean that he was dead wrong.

There is an antinuclear national organization called Physicians for Social Responsibility (whose president, pediatrician Helen Caldicott, has achieved great fame and attention, even though she knows as much about nuclear weapons as I do about pediatrics) that has informed millions and millions of Americans that adequate medical care for nuclear-war casualties would be impossible. Coming straight from the horse's mouth, this body of belief has had considerable effect on U.S. public opinion—including the professor's opinion, since he shared the organization's apocalyptic view of nuclear war. Since this view most probably is in serious error, any claims of a societal collapse because physical survivors will

125

have inadequate medical care are most probably in serious error. But knowledge of this is not about to change most people's minds on the matter, especially when the physicians themselves feel this way.

Without a doubt, the most feared effect of nuclear weapons is radioactive fallout. (Remember the ghastly scenes in *The Day After* of fallout coming down and corpses strewn over the countryside covered with radioactive "snow"?) Even were most people able physically to survive fallout by occupying civil defense shelters, what will their behavior be when they surface and try to live in an environment of low-level radioactive contamination? (By low-level radioactive contamination, I'm referring to a level which, while not absolutely safe, will be less life threatening than the perils we normally subject ourselves to in the form of cigarette smoking, coal burning, chemical waste disposal, automobile driving, etc.) I can't answer this question in any objective way, except to say that even a grossly unrealistic fear is still a fear; and that it's possible that our society might go berserk under these conditions. I suspect that my psychologist acquaintance would say that it's highly probable. But who am I to challenge him on his own turf!

What I'm driving at here is that in an unpredictable world full of unpredictable human beings, there is simply no possible way to resolve the issue of surviving nuclear war by trying to be knowledgeable and technically factual. Our ignorance on this issue so far exceeds our understanding and factuality that one is grossly deceiving himself if he thinks that logic can have much impact on the issue. In this respect, while I hope that what I've written in the preceding chapters sounds logical to you, in no way have I written on the expectation that I would convert you to my beliefs. At a maximum I hoped that I might stir your thinking a bit by presenting the subject material in a way you might not have seen before. If I have seemed deeply set in my beliefs, which may have conflicted with yours, it's not because I can defend them to the last letter. Rather, it's because the issue is too important not to have beliefs on, and I felt that my beliefs were important enough to express to you.

On the other hand, what I'm trying to say in this final chapter is that if most of us (that is, most Americans) adhere to the belief that nuclear war is not survivable (however we define "survivable," which is so highly subjective a term), then in the long run we will not survive as a free nation. A fatalistic fear of the consequences of nuclear war will erode our national will to resist the designs the

Soviets have for bringing us into their orbit. Sooner or later such an attitude will make us vulnerable to Soviet threats and intimidation and we will find ourselves increasingly bowing to their will and coming under their control.

At issue here is not a case of "Better Red than dead." Rather, it is a matter of being horrified less over the consequences of a communist takeover than over the assumed horrors of the aftermath of nuclear war—the horrors of *The Day After* and the years after that. We seem to be confronted with a Scylla and Charybdis predicament, except that the two monsters may not both be mythological.

Based on the longstanding record of Soviet repression and brutality in countries that have fallen under their domination (to say nothing about the USSR itself), living under Soviet control, there is little doubt, would be a horrifying experience for most Americans. A Soviet Scylla almost certainly would be a monstrous fact, not a mythological fiction. How monstrous Soviet domination might be, let us hope we never find out. I would point out, however, that before the United States was seriously threatened with nuclear war, the American people were mainly of a mind to go along with Patrick Henry: "Give me liberty or give me death." But now this appears to have changed, because of the threat of nuclear war.

Today there is a widespread (maybe even prevailing) dread that we may not have the simple choice of liberty or death. If we were willing to fight a nuclear war in defense of our liberty, those who did not die might wish that they had. As a renowned nuclear strategist, the late Herman Kahn, used to ask, "Will the living envy the dead?" A loss of political liberty might be preferred to the assumed hell of being alive in the aftermath of nuclear war. Which brings up the nuclear Charybdis side of the dilemma and whether the assumption of nuclear hell long before a merciful death may be more mythology than fact.

As I have attempted to point out, the Soviets seem to be concerned with avoiding a nuclear hell for the country with whom they might have to fight a nuclear war. They are concerned more with imposing the blessings of communism on the liberated American masses than with making their life a nuclear hell on earth. As I also have attempted to point out, if we were to place maximum effort on defending ourselves against nuclear attack, whatever the effects of the enemy's attack might be, they could be very substantially reduced. Combining these two factors, with their impli-

127

cations for our "survival" in nuclear war, no one can say that there will be an aftermath of such hellish dimensions as to be ruled intolerable by most people in advance.

As to how tolerable or intolerable a nuclear war aftermath might be, assuming that we had done everything possible to protect ourselves, there is only one way of finding out: have a nuclear war and then see what happens to our societal fabric—not an ideal way of proving or disproving an argument. And even then, who in heaven's name would be interested in making evaluations and judgments when a nuclear war—bound to be a horrible experience—has just erupted. The judgment has to be made now by the American people, based on whether they are willing to face the issue, educate themselves on the basic facts of the matter, and decide on taking a chance on survival by trying to survive. They dare not write the matter off as hopeless, which is what their political leaders and most of the media have long been telling them.

We must face the issue and make up our own minds on how to resolve it. Our political leaders, for political reasons, are not about to show any leadership and help us resolve it. The Soviets almost certainly will not help us by helping to eliminate nuclear stockpiles through arms-control negotiations. We will have to make our own way out of this mess in which we have so foolishly mired ourselves.

Can we face the issue? I don't know. That's up to the American people to decide. I would like to say, like a good politician, that I have faith in my country and in my countrymen, and that we will. But I can't, because there is so little in our record on nuclear-weapons matters to indicate that we will. If we don't, however, for all the reasons I have tried to spell out here, we will be facing a future far more perilous than it need have been. A future we may not survive.

NOTES

Chapter 1

1. Speech to the United Press International luncheon, Chicago, 5 May, 1981.
2. Speech, "NATO—The Next Thirty Years," Brussels, Belgium, 1 Sept., 1979.
3. Gen. A. S. Milovidov and Col. V. G. Koslov, eds., "The Philosophical Heritage of V. I. Lenin and Problems of Contemporary War" (Moscow, 1972).
4. Speech to the Sandia Corporation Colloquium on Tactical Nuclear Weapons, Albuquerque, N.M., Oct. 1965.
5. "Toward a New Defense for NATO" (National Strategy Information Center, New York, 1976).

Chapter 2

1. Gen. Bernard Rogers, "The Atlantic Alliance: Prescriptions for a Difficult Decade," *Foreign Affairs*, Summer, 1982.
2. Ibid.
3. Robert S. McNamara, "The Military Role of Nuclear Weapons," *Foreign Affairs*, Fall, 1983.

Chapter 3

1. "Report of the Secretary of Defense Caspar W. Weinberger to the Congress," 1 Feb., 1983.

Chapter 4

1. A. A. Grechko, "The Armed Forces of the Soviet State" (Moscow, 1974).

Chapter 5

1. Carl Sagan, "Nuclear War and Climatic Catastrophe: Some Policy Implications," *Foreign Affairs*, Winter, 1983–84.